WITH A DREAM SO PROUD

The Life of Stephen Vincent Benét

By

Donnell Rubay

The opinions expressed in this manuscript are solely the opinions of the author and do not represent the opinions or thoughts of the publisher. The author has represented and warranted full ownership and/or legal right to publish all the materials in this book.

With A Dream So Proud:
The Life of Stephen Vincent Benét
By Donnell Rubay
All Rights Reserved
Copyright @2016 Donnell Rubay
Published by Benicia Literary Arts
www.benicialiteraryarts.org
Benicia, California

ISBN 978-0-9703737-5-5
Library of Congress Control Number 2016946257

Produced by Benicia Literary Arts, which encourages reading and writing in the community by producing events, creating a community of writers and readers, encouraging their development, and publishing works of high quality in all genres. The website is www.BeniciaLiteraryArts.org.

Editor: Mary Eichbauer
Layout: Lois Requist

Cover Art: Angela Hanlon

Quotations from the writings of Stephen Vincent Benét and Benét family photographs courtesy of Thomas C. Benét. Used by permission. All rights reserved.

Every effort has been made to obtain required permissions. If a permission has been overlooked, please contact the publisher, and it will be corrected in future editions.

This book may not be reproduced, transmitted, or stored in whole or in part by any means, including graphic, electronic, or mechanical, without the express written consent of the publisher except in the case of brief quotations in critical articles and reviews.

To Tom Benét, of course.

Major Works By Stephen Vincent Benét

Prose

The Beginning of Wisdom (1921)—Novel
Young People's Pride (1922)—Novel
Jean Huguenot (1923)—Novel
Spanish Bayonet (1926)—Novel
James Shore's Daughter (1934)—Novel
Thirteen O'clock (1937)—Short stories
Tales Before Midnight (1939)—Short stories
Cheers for Miss Bishop (1941)—Screenplay
America (1944)—Nonfiction
We Stand United (1945)—Radio Scripts
The Last Circle (1946)—Short stories

Poetry

Five Men and Pompey (1915)
The Drug Shop or Endymion in Edmonstoun (1917)
Young Adventure (1918)
"The Mountain Whippoorwill: Or How Hill-Billy Jim Won the Great Fiddler's Prize" (1925)
Tiger Joy (1925)
Heavens and Earth (1920)
John Brown's Body (1928)—Pulitzer Prize, Poetry
Ballads and Poems (1931)
A Book of Americans (with Rosemary Benét) (1933)
Nightmare at Noon (1942)
They Burned the Books (1942)
Western Star (unfinished) (1944)—Pulitzer Prize, Poetry

Selected Works

Volume One: Poetry (1942)
Volume Two: Prose (1942)

Short stories

"An End to Dreams" (1932)—O. Henry Award, First Place Prize
"The Sobbin' Women" (1937)—Movie Musical: *Seven Brides for Seven Brothers* (1954)
"The Devil and Daniel Webster" (1937)—O. Henry Award, First Place Prize; Movies: *The Devil and Daniel Webster,* also called *All That Money Can Buy* (1941) and *Shortcut to Happiness* (2003)
"Johnny Pye and the Fool-Killer" (1938)—Musical (1993)
"Freedom is a Hard Bought Thing" (1940)—O. Henry Award, First Place Prize
"Famous" (1946)—Movie: *Just for You* (1952)

Short Nonfiction

"A Creed for Americans" Written for the Council for Democracy (1942)
"The American Dream" *The Country Gentleman* (November 1942)
"Freedom From Fear" *The Saturday Evening Post* (March 13, 1943)

Your John Brown's Body *is my favorite poem, my favorite book. I know more of it by heart than I do any other poetry. It means more to me, is realer than anything I've ever read by any poet, bar none, and I've read an awful lot of poetry.* . . .

    Margaret Mitchell, author of *Gone With the Wind*, in a 1936 letter to Stephen Vincent Benét[1]

PRELUDE[a]

Jabez Stone had a problem. He'd just sold his soul to the Devil. It'd been so easy: a quick vow, an offer to take two cents for the thing. How was he to know the Devil would accept?

Later, he'd tried to argue his way out of the deal. "Look Devil, sir. Times were tough, the kids were sick, the wife was sick, there were rocks in the cornfield and the money was just about gone—the thing is, you gotta know—I didn't really mean it."

The Devil, a tall man in a black suit with very sharp white teeth, smiled before saying, in his slow, deep voice: "I'm sorry, but a deal's a deal."

Poor Jabez, he was about frantic when he heard this. And, making matters worse, he saw a tiny creature flutter from the devil's clutches, a creature that looked like a moth but was not a moth. "Help me!" the creature cried, and Jabez knew the creature was a human soul who, like Jabez, had made a deal with the devil.

When Jabez first made the deal, there had been no problem—in fact, quite the opposite. For not only did his children and his wife recover from their sickness, but the rocks disappeared from his cornfield, and he was having so much good fortune that he soon became one of the richest men in the county.

But what good was all Jabez's success, if the devil owned his soul? And the devil clearly had the right to Jabez's soul, for the creature had carefully kept the written agreement, signed with Jabez's blood.

Was there no way Jabez could escape his fate?

Now, Stephen Vincent Benét, the author of Jabez's story, had a problem: how could he free Jabez Stone from the devil's clutches? And this problem was on top of the larger one that had prompted Stephen to begin Jabez's story in the first place: the problem of having no money, mounting debts and a wife and three children to support. [b]

Facing Jabez Stone's dilemma, Stephen would realize what it was that gave him—and every human—the strength, the will, the desire, to forge ahead in a world of hardships. This knowledge would come from the wisdom gained, and experiences weathered, in Stephen's own life. A life that began back in Bethlehem, Pennsylvania, when an Army captain named James Walker Benét and his wife Frances Rose were expecting their third child.

Before Stephen could create Jabez, he had to create himself.

---

a. This "Prelude" includes a retelling of a portion of the Stephen Vincent Benét short story "The Devil and Daniel Webster." It contains paraphrases of the dialogue in that story, ***not*** accurate quotations.

b. In April, 1935, just before Stephen began writing about Jabez Stone, he wrote in his diary: "Hand to mouth for last 3 ½ years. . . [And] still going on. Should be used to it but am not—takes my courage now. You lose, in time, the first flair, when it is exciting to be broke, [and are able to] work days at a stretch, and redeem finances by some coup." (Fenton 291) In July, 1935 Stephen added: "Try to work on story in evening but no go. Owe lots of money. Am so tired of things being like that." (Fenton 292)

Mother I am really very fond of already. The old man says, "I am the child of his old age." My mother thinks I am too sweet. I heard her say so. Thank heaven, here comes afternoon tea and I need it in my business.

The baby Stephen, as interpreted by his father[2]

PART ONE: A BOY CALLED "TIBS"

Frances Rose Benét was going to have a baby, and she was terrified. It was 1898, and seven of every hundred mothers died in childbirth. The older the woman, the more likely she was to die. And Frances was not young. Her son William was twelve, and her daughter Laura was fourteen.

"You're healthy," the doctor reassured her. "Don't worry, you'll be fine."

The thing about death from childbirth in 1898 was that many of the women who died from it had been healthy, right up until the baby was born. Complications during delivery—more common with older mothers—could lead to excessive bleeding and other problems. Also, before doctors and midwives fully understood the importance of cleanliness, and before bacteria-killing antibiotics had been discovered, bacteria were a real danger.

There was another problem: most babies in 1898 were not born in hospitals but in the family's home. Hospitals were not places to be born, but places to die. The high risk of contracting bacteria in a hospital made them particularly dangerous.[3] Yet the Benét family had no home at the moment. The father, James Walker Benét, was a captain in the U.S Army and had not yet been assigned to his latest post. Until then, the family was living in a hotel in Bethlehem, Pennsylvania.

Obviously, Frances could not make herself any younger. Maybe, however, the baby would not have to be born in a hotel.

On a bright morning in early summer, with the leaves of the red maples glistening in the sun, Frances was browsing the shops along Bethlehem's main street. Somewhere between a tearoom and a hat shop she encountered her cousin, Mrs. Colby. The two women greeted each other happily, Frances learning that Mrs. Colby lived in nearby Fountain Hill, and Mrs. Colby learning that Frances was to soon have a baby—in a hotel.

"We cannot have that," Mrs. Colby said. "And a solution is simple. My husband and I are off to New York in a week. Your family can have my house and my two good maids, for the entire summer."[4]

Therefore, Stephen Vincent Benét was born, on July 22, 1898, in a comfortable home in Fountain Hill, Pennsylvania.[5] And, despite her fears, Frances survived the birth quite easily.

Father, James Walker Benét and Mother, Frances Rose Benét

Within months of his youngest child's birth, Captain Benét was posted to the United States Army Arsenal in the town of Watervliet, New York.[6] In an arsenal, the Army stores "ordnance"—things like weapons, ammunition, combat vehicles, and even camels (but only for a short time in the 1800s; someone thought they'd be helpful in desert battles.)

Army arsenals were part of the history of the Benét family. Captain Benét's father, also named Stephen Vincent Benét, had been a brigadier general and the commander of all the army arsenals in the United States. During the Civil War, General Stephen Vincent Benét had been in charge of all the ordnance used by the Union Army.

Probably the most important weapon stored in an arsenal in the early 1900s was the "16-inch gun." This gun, in fact, was the reason Captain Benét was sent to Watervliet: his job there would be to supervise the production of these giant guns.

At the time, before airplanes could carry bombs, these guns were among the most dangerous weapons available. The gun was called a "16-inch gun" because the barrel was 16 inches wide—just the right size to hold a small child for a photograph (as photographs of young Stephen prove).[7] The gun itself was huge—as long as half a football field and weighing over 385,000 pounds. With a gun like this an army could shoot a 2,370-pound missile about 21 miles; shooting off such a gun at Yankee Stadium could topple the Statue of Liberty.[8]

Though she lived much of her life in army arsenals, Stephen's mother rarely thought about guns.In the early 1900s, her thoughts were focused on Stephen, her youngest son, who had taken to calling himself "Tibbie"—or "Tibs" for short.[9]

Unfortunately, Stephen was a worry because he was so often ill. In the years before antibiotics and other drugs, infectious diseases that are often curable today, like pneumonia and flu, were deadly. Even diarrhea was a major killer. Stephen did not settle for a common disease, though.

The Benét Family home in Watervliet

His first major illness was scarlet fever, and, though he survived the disease, it left him with weak eyes, requiring him to wear thick glasses throughout his life.[10]

A few years after Stephen's bout with scarlet fever, Captain Benét, now a major, was transferred to the army arsenal in Rock Island, Illinois. Frances knew that Rock Island had recently suffered an outbreak of polio—a dangerous disease that, even if it did not kill, could leave its victims paralyzed. Her two older children, Laura and William, were safe living at their boarding schools, but five-year-old Stephen, weakened by his bout of scarlet fever—well, she simply refused to take him to such a dangerous place.

So, while her husband headed to Rock Island alone, Frances took Stephen with her to Carlisle, Pennsylvania, to stay with her mother. Stephen would later describe Carlisle as "the kind of place where storybook grandmothers *ought* to live." Stephen would go on to explain: the "funny . . . and quaint" town had "brick paths and wide streets with big shady trees all along them," while the people lived in "red-brick houses with scrubbed doorsteps and little white houses covered with vines."[11]

Shortly after arriving in Carlisle, however, Stephen promptly caught typhoid fever, another life-threatening illness. The disease, spread by bacteria, left Stephen weak and with severe stomach pain.[12] Frances may have blamed herself, for Stephen probably got the disease from drinking contaminated water or eating unwashed fruit.

For months, Frances nursed her youngest child through the course of his illness, all the while worrying that—after young Stephen recovered—she might eventually have to move the two of them to Rock Island anyway. A wife's place was with her husband, but how could she take Stephen to a place where he risked catching polio?

Stephen in a 16-inch gun.

She was rescued from this dilemma because Major Benét's stay in Rock Island turned out to be short. In early 1905 he was given his first command: an appointment as Commanding Officer of the Army Arsenal in Benicia, a small city near the San Francesco Bay, in California.[13]

The entire family was excited about the move to California. The major headed to California first, while Frances and Stephen waited for Laura and William to return from school. Waiting with them was Frances' seventy-one-year-old aunt, Agnes Mahan. Typical of the time, since it was difficult for women to find employment to support themselves, unmarried female relatives often lived with family members.

The long cross-country trip, according to Stephen's sister Laura, would make a permanent impression on seven-year-old Stephen. Completely recovered from the typhoid, Stephen was entranced by the scenery flashing past the train windows. Flat farm fields green with new growth gave way to miles of dry desert, sprinkled with cacti and the bones of animals. As the train approached California, it stopped in the bustling sunbaked town of Reno, Nevada, before climbing through the mighty Sierra Nevada—the very mountains in which the Donner Party had been stranded and starved, back in covered wagon days. Perhaps most exciting was the stop in Auburn, California, an actual gold-mining town, where miners still walked the streets in their heavy boots and cowboy hats.

Mrs. Benét made sure all her children understood what they were seeing as the train rolled along. On a little platform at the end of the train she gathered her family to tell them stories set in the places they were seeing. "That is the Great Salt Lake; there are the towering Rocky Mountains," she might have told them. On the last morning, the children had a special treat out on that platform—a breakfast of fresh-caught mountain trout and just-picked raspberries.[14]

Laura would later write of Stephen that he "was deeply and powerfully interested in his America, her legends, her songs, her explorers, her public men." And this first cross-country trip triggered that deep interest, an interest—really a love—that would seep into much of the poetry and many of the stories he would later write.[15] As an adult, one of Stephen's favorite short-story topics was America's history, while his last great work was an effort to describe America's westward movement.[16]

***

Arriving in Benicia, Stephen saw his new home for the first time: a two-story pillared mansion sitting on a point of land surrounded on three sides by the waters of the Carquinez Strait. Stephen would later describe the place as "the big house with the big porch and all California outside."[17]

A sweeping lawn dotted with magnolia and palm trees spread around the house. An avenue of cork oaks and eucalyptus led past it, and roses were "everywhere," while fruit trees were so plentiful that Stephen was soon eating seven oranges a day directly from the gardens.[18]

"It wasn't like an arsenal," wrote a family friend after a visit. "It was like the backdrop of a romantic play, all pepper trees and acacias and fountains and pillared porches."[19]

For his family's first meal in their new home, the major had ordered something special, a food of California's Spanish and Mexican heritage: hot tamales. To the new arrivals dining on the exotic tamales, the world they'd left behind in the East seemed very far away.[20]

"The big house with the big porch and all California outside."

In his new post, Major Benét had found a comfortable fit, not to mention year-round California sunshine. As the commander of an arsenal, he could serve his country in an important post while avoiding war and violence. The major believed war was justified only if necessary to protect the peace or national security. He was liked and respected by the men he led, who saw that he truly lived the military creed of duty, honor, country,[21] and that he never asked his men to do what he would not.[22]

Mrs. Benét enjoyed arsenal life because it allowed her to spend time with her husband, as well as providing her with the society of officers' wives for teas and outings.

For Aunt Agnes, life in a household with a young boy, particularly one who had recently adopted a curly haired spaniel named Prince, could be trying. There was the running up and down stairs of boy and dog, accompanied by loud barking and shouts. And then the disagreements with that young man: for example, Stephen often had to inform his aunt—quite firmly—that Prince had absolutely no *trace* of smell.[23]

One summer when Laura was home from college, she and Stephen rode the train into the California gold-rush country to see the gold mines and rivers up close.[24] On another occasion, the family took the two-hour ferry ride to visit San Francisco, just thirty miles away. The proud owner of a new camera, Laura took pictures of the people on the streets for the family photo album.[25]

For Stephen there was the special freedom of no school!

In the early 1900's, Benicia was a vibrant community of factories—leather tanneries and fish canneries—shops, and dairies, but few of its citizens had college educations or planned to send their children to college. The Benéts did not feel the local schools were sufficiently academic for their youngest son. A better education for Stephen, they believed, could be provided by themselves. Obtaining lessons from the Calvert's Correspondence System, the major supervised mathematics lessons, and Laura, once she moved back home after college, took over supervision of the other subjects.[26] For several years, this home-schooling worked fine. Once Stephen's academic needs grew beyond what could be provided by his life in the Arsenal—then, there might be a problem.

***

Laura, Stephen and William

The Benéts had been in their new home for barely a year when they were awakened one morning by the earth rumbling beneath them, while the walls of the house shook. Later that day they learned that the city of San Francesco had been shaken by a violent earthquake and was now being consumed by fire. That evening Stephen could even see an eerie red glow caused by the fire, low in the sky to the west.[27] Major Benét's first concern was for the lives of everyone in the Arsenal, since the entire place—as a storage area for weapons—ran the risk of exploding if jostled too strongly by an aftershock.[28]

The family also learned that the quake had trapped several San Francescans in their upstairs bedrooms—walls had shifted, jamming doors, and staircases had crumbled. Fearful of becoming trapped by an aftershock, for many days after the quake everyone in the Benét family sat up all night in the great room downstairs.[29]

During a visit to San Francisco before the quake, Stephen's big brother William, now almost 20, had met a young bookstore clerk named Teresa Thompson who had several brothers and sisters. Teresa's older sister was named Kathleen and the younger one was Margaret. When William invited Teresa out to Benicia, her sisters came along.

The Thompson children had recently lost both of their parents, so Kathleen and Teresa had thrown themselves into raising their younger siblings. From their first meeting, Mrs. Benét adored the sisters. She admired the strength of the older girls in handling their job as substitute parents, and the great love all the siblings had for each other. Yearning to share her own love with the family, Mrs. Benét had the girls call her "Mother Bun," and the Benét family presented the sisters with a small gold key in a quilted box, the key "to the Benéts' hearts forever."

Kathleen later described the games the Benéts and Thompsons often played in the great room of the Benét home. Some of the games were early versions of Trivial Pursuit, though far more challenging. For example, the questions might offer a line of poetry, then ask for the poem it came from, or provide a famous quotation and ask the name of the speaker. Another game involved the contestants, including young Stephen, attempting to write sonnets in the style of a fourteenth-century Italian poet named Petrarch.

Kathleen Thompson, under the name "Kathleen Norris," would later write more than ninety novels, many of them romances and most of them best sellers.[30]

Other visitors included William's male friends. Leonard Bacon had attended Yale, as had William, and was now a popular professor at the nearby University of California in Berkeley. A student would describe him in her yearbook as "English prof—charming."[31] In 1940 Bacon would win the Pulitzer Prize for Poetry.

Another Yale friend of William's, who stayed with the Benéts the entire summer of 1909, was nicknamed Sinclair "Red" Lewis for his bright red hair. Though Lewis would later be the first American author to win the Nobel Prize for literature, during his Benicia summer he lost many a tennis match to eleven-year-old Stephen.[32] That fall, Lewis moved to San Francesco to work as a reporter for the Associated Press. Early Christmas morning he returned to his San Francisco room, planning to catch the 7 a.m. train to join the Benéts in Benicia, when he found a box from them, bursting with gifts. Having nothing to give those "absolutely wonderful Benéts . . . the DEARS" he quickly typed up several of his recent poems, slipped them between two pieces of leather, and bound the whole thing with a ribbon.[33] Now he had a gift to give the family.

Stephen's favorite visitor was his brother William, whom he adored. In his older brother, young Stephen saw all his heroes, including Perseus, a heroic monster-slaying son of the Greek god Zeus; D'Artagnan, one of the Three Musketeers; and Lancelot, knight of King Arthur's Camelot.[34]

When Stephen was lucky enough to have William to himself, Stephen would steal nickels from his piggy bank so that the two could ride the *Solano* ferry. The *Solano* was huge, the largest ferry in the world—425 feet long (more than 100 feet longer than a football field). It carried the entire Southern Pacific train—forty-eight train cars, one locomotive and all the passengers—from Benicia, across the Carquinez Strait, to the town of Port Costa. Stephen adored the delicious corn muffins sold in the ferry's restaurant. Finding space on a wooden bench, Stephen would savor bites of his muffin while watching the tourists from the East Coast—the men in caps and overcoats, the women draped with furs—and think about how stuffy and boring they all looked.[35] Though Stephen would one day live in the East himself, he would retain the habit of viewing the people around him as different—more stuffy and boring—than himself.

***

During the quiet times, when no visitors shared the house, when even Laura and William were away, Stephen could still be content. It was during these times he'd be most likely to get a walk with his father, when they could talk about his grandfathers, both of whom had fought in the Civil War. Or he might play with his toy soldiers; he owned over 400 of them, all carefully catalogued.[36] And without others to disturb him, Stephen could spend hours reading.

Stephen loved reading, a love that had developed so early in his life that to him it was almost as basic as breathing. Once, back when he was two or three, Mrs. Benét had discovered him on the nursery floor "reading" aloud, though the book was upside down. "Stephen—what are you doing?" she'd asked.

"Why, I'm reading to that mouse," he informed her, though he was sure it was quite obvious, for there *was* a small mouse resting quietly beside him. The fact that the mouse had been caught in a trap and was quite dead did not concern him.[37]

Luckily—because Stephen loved to read—Major Benét had acquired a large collection of books. With no public library yet in Benicia, the books the family owned would have been the only books Stephen could read. As Stephen grew from the ages of seven to twelve, he worked through his father's books—one day reading military reports, while the next puzzling over the poetry of Dante, returning frequently to *Battles and Leaders of the Civil War*, as well as devouring science fiction. Once, when he was nine, a search of the family library uncovered a play by a man named William Shakespeare. At dinner that evening Stephen reported his discovery, then said: "I like that man's writing, has he written anything else?"[38]

Stephen's favorite books contained adventure and took him to far-away places. Alexander Dumas's tales of swashbuckling sword fights, like *The Three Musketeers*,[39] were reread many times. California writer Jack London, who had braved the snows of Alaska while gold mining, captured Stephen's imagination with his best-selling story about Buck, a sled dog who hears *The Call of the Wild*. Still another Stephen favorite was poet and short-story writer Rudyard Kipling, whose *Jungle Book*—reincarnated many years later as two Disney movies—was a popular collection of animal escapades set in India. In order to get in all the reading he wanted, Stephen often huddled under his covers at night with a story long after he was supposed to be sleeping.[40]

Occasionally, Stephen received books from writer friends of Laura or William. That's how he obtained an early copy of *Hike and the Aeroplane*, the first novel by his old tennis opponent Sinclair Lewis, writing under the pen name "Tom Graham." In the story, 16-year-old Gerald "Hike" Griffin and his best friend Torrington "Poodle" Darby attend the Santa Benicia Military Academy, in the town of Santa Benicia. In creating town and academy, Lewis used a place where he had been happy—the Benicia Arsenal in the town of Benicia—as his model. Very likely he also had young Stephen in mind as his first boy-reader.

In the book, Hike and Poodle stumble upon an amazing flying machine and its inventor, Martin Priest. The boys then agree to fly the plane across the country to Washington, D.C., to see if the United States government might buy the plane for the Army. Because the book was written only nine years after the Wright Brothers' first flight, Mr. Priest's flying machine seemed truly amazing.

In 1911, just before the Benéts left Bencia, the city got its first public library. So when Stephen wrote Lewis a fan letter about *Hike and the Aeroplane* he was able to say:

Cover of *Hike and the Aeroplane*

> It's swell . . . one of the best boy books this year, indeed the best Are you going to write a sequel? I guess you are for you let the villain escape! Miss Granicle who has been visiting us says she will present a copy to the Benicia Library. So you see how famous you are![41]

As with reading, Stephen had felt—at a young age—a longing to write, and not just with a pen or pencil. At the age of three, when asked what he'd like for Christmas, he'd said, "A typewriter."[42]

He didn't get the typewriter until he was seven, a few months after he'd arrived in Benicia. While waiting, he wrote three short stories, longhand, on Benicia Arsenal letterhead. One of them, called "Mr. Progg's Conversion," tells the story of a drinking man, Mr. Progg, who comes home one day to find a green cat. His wife had painted the cat, hoping to scare her husband into mending his ways. When Mr. Progg sees the green cat he is terrified, believing he is going crazy, and never takes another drink. [43]

After the precious typewriter became his, Stephen typed several poems, one of which discusses the pros and cons of marriage:

MARRYING

Why do you want a   wife

you'l be wreched all your

life mabye so said the

man but she can make

good   fudge in a pan

Stephen V Benét Benicia

Arsenal Benicia Cal

With the ability to write stories as good as "Mr. Progg's Conversion" and poems as clever as "Marrying," Stephen was sure he'd soon be ready to publish in the magazines.

Grandfather Stephen Vincent Benét and Grandmother Laura Walker Benét

For Stephen, as a child longing to write, it helped that writing ran in the family. Grandfather Benét had written and translated several military books,[45] including his translation from the French of a book about Napoleon's defeat in the Battle of Waterloo in the early 1800s, a battle that remained famous for decades.[46] In fact, General Benét had used his writing skills to court Stephen's future grandmother, Laura Walker. Then-Lieutenant Benét gave Miss Walker a copy of his book inscribed from "her friend."[47]

Both William and Laura also loved writing. In later life, Laura would publish stories and biographies for young people, while William would publish novels and poetry.

Stephen's father, elevated to lieutenant colonel in the summer of 1907, was an authority on English literature and poetry. Many a warm evening the family and their guests would gather on the leafy front porch to talk about people and books. The colonel, handsome in his white uniform, with mint juleps on a side table, offered well-meant words of wisdom. During the summer of 1909, for example, the colonel and Sinclair Lewis had long, intense debates about life, politics, literature, and an array of other topics. When the subject turned to a philosophical manuscript Lewis was working on, the colonel called it "a whole mess of claptrap" and suggested Lewis replace the thing with the couplet: "Do the things you cannot do / so your soul shall grow."[48] (Lewis may have heeded the colonel's advice, since the "claptrap" was never published.) Years later, Stephen would remember his father's voice floating out into the warm evening until Stephen became too sleepy to listen.[49]

Colonel Benét even dabbled in poetry himself. When William was in kindergarten, his father wrote a rhyme about the little girl on whom William had a crush:

> My admiration never tires
> For the lovely Sarah Myers.
> When her nose began to bleed,
> I felt very sad indeed. [50]

While the colonel enjoyed humorous poetry, he had a special soft spot for poetry that was unintentionally bad. From his reading, the colonel collected examples of this type of poetry in a notebook he called *Minus Poetry*—a collection to which Stephen added as he grew older.[51] A favorite practice of the colonel's was to bring out this collection to share with unsuspecting guests.

In her autobiography, *Family Gathering*, Kathleen Thompson Norris recalled thinking that the colonel might have been happier as a writer, entering the Army only because that was what the men in the Benét family did, going back two hundred years. Eerily, she also wrote about Colonel Benét "half-seriously" complaining that since all three of his children had poetic gifts, the financial future of the family looked dim. Could it be that the colonel had glimpsed the future?

Eventually, poetry became Stephen's favorite form of writing and he was writing it every chance he could get. For his sister's birthday he wrote a poem about her horse Nettie, then used it to wrap a second gift, a horseshoe-shaped brooch. [52]

Shortly after his own twelfth birthday in 1910, Stephen saw a poem he'd written in print for the first time. He won a contest sponsored by *St. Nicholas Magazine*, a popular monthly children's magazine. In addition to seeing his poem in print, Stephen was awarded three dollars; with books for boys selling at 50 cents each and candy bars costing only a penny, this was a princely sum. The title of his winning poem was "The Regret of Dives"—a rather strange name, but he'd had to use the word "dives" because he needed a rhyme for "hives."[53]

Also in 1910, the Benét family hosted a wedding. The youngest Thompson sister, Margaret, became engaged to a Navy ensign named Charles Hartigan, stationed at nearby Mare Island Naval Base in Vallejo. One night Hartigan's ship was ordered to sail within two days, upsetting the existing wedding plans. Undaunted, the Benéts went to work. The next morning the entire Benét family, including twelve-year-old Stephen, rode a horse-drawn surrey to the county seat to get the marriage license. Next it was back to Benicia for the wedding in the local Catholic church, with the colonel walking Margaret down the aisle and Laura serving as bridesmaid. Afterwards, everyone returned to the Benét home for a wedding breakfast. [54]

There was a shadow darkening the sunny California days, however: Stephen had outgrown his home-schooling. Also, no other children Stephen's age lived near the Benéts, who were located out in the army arsenal a mile from the town. To learn to socialize with his peers, Stephen needed to be with other children. It was time for Stephen to attend school.

Yet the suggestion to send Stephen to school did not come from any of the Benéts. Interestingly, it was the family doctor who voiced the concern. Perhaps, as someone outside the family who also had the family's respect, he was in a good position to point out Stephen's need for greater social and academic challenges. [55]

The family doctor recommended boarding school, but Mrs. Benét was not ready to part with her youngest son. Instead she redoubled her efforts to educate Stephen.

As for socializing with children his own age, Mrs. Benét attempted to fill this gap as well. First, she tried incorporating lessons into games, one of which was called "Animal Peculiarities." As Colonel Benét described this effort in a letter to Laura: "You should have seen your mother impersonating a seal. She'd dive right off her chair."[56]

A cover of *St. Nicholas Magazine* in 1910.

For an outdoor activity, Mrs. Benét purchased a donkey and a cart. The donkey, named Teddy, was rather stubborn. Sometimes he'd simply lie down in the road and refuse to budge, or he might be in a jumpy mood. One day he was so jumpy, he tossed Mrs. Benét out of the cart! Mrs. Benét was stubborn as well; she was not going to free Teddy from his job of pulling the cart.

Instead, she asked her husband to assign a soldier the duty of taking Stephen for a daily ride in the cart.

For several weeks Stephen and a gruff, but friendly, soldier named Henry made daily visits to town in the cart hitched to Teddy. The arrangement might have continued except that, one day, a woman from town walked the long mile to the commanding officer's house and paid a call on Mrs. Benét. Ushered into the great mansion, and then into the presence of the commanding officer's wife, the woman almost lost her nerve. Yet she'd come too far to turn back. Shyly, she told Mrs. Benét that a donkey and an empty cart stood outside the town's most popular saloon for an hour every day.

Stephen with donkey and cart.

"My," Mrs. Benét replied in surprise, "surely it was not my son's donkey and cart."

"Well," the visitor retorted, slightly miffed by Mrs. Benét's reaction. "No other child in Benicia has a donkey and cart."

Shortly after the visitor had left, Mrs. Benét cornered Stephen: "Has Henry been stopping at the saloons?" she asked.

What could Stephen say? He didn't want his mother to think Henry was not doing his duty, because that was not the case. "Henry does take me to the saloon . . ." he began, searching his mind for the best words. Suddenly, he knew: "But Henry doesn't abandon me. While he drinks his beer he gives me a pile of nickels so I can play the slot machines."

Needless to say, that was the end of Henry, Teddy, and the cart. [57]

But the doctor remained concerned that Stephen needed more rigorous schooling and more companions his own age. His recommendation? The Hitchcock Military Academy, a boarding school in the city of San Rafael, California, several hours from Benicia by ferry.

Academically, the school was rigorous. All students wore military uniforms and spent part of their time marching in military formation. Stephen had challenging classes in mathematics, English, history, science, and classical languages like Greek and Latin. Yet he did so well he was able to skip the eighth grade. [58]

Hitchcock marked him in unexpected ways. For the rest of his life, Stephen rarely spoke of his time at the school. One mention is in a poem he wrote in college about a young boy returning to boarding school and re-encountering a bully. As the ferry arrives at the school, there, straight ahead,

> Were dock and fellows. Stumbling, he was whirled
> Out and away to meet them—and his back
> Slumped to the old half-cringe, his hands fell slack;
> A big boy's arm went round him—and a twist
> Sent shattering pain along his tortured wrist,
> As a voice cried, a bloated voice and fat,
> "Why it's Miss Nancy! Come along, you rat!"[59]

Stephen never blamed his parents for sending him to Hitchcock, for he understood that they'd only been trying to do what was best for him, with few options to choose from. If forced to talk about Hitchcock, he was careful to say that he was grateful to the school for giving him a broader view of the world—not everyone enjoys poetry, not everyone is nice. He understood that the experience of pain and hardship could create a sensitivity to the pain and hardship others might feel. Such empathy very likely helped him to become a better writer, as well as a wiser person.

Stephen's time at Hitchcock was brief—little more than a year. In the summer of 1911, Colonel Benét was promoted to full colonel and assigned to the Ordnance Training Corps at Camp Hancock in Augusta, Georgia. [60]

But, even in the lion's cage, in Zoos
You'll find a sparrow, picking up the crumbs
And taking life precisely as it comes.

From "Sparrow"[61]

PART TWO: TEENAGER

During the summer of 1911, shortly before Stephen's thirteenth birthday, he boarded his second cross-country train. This time, however, he was traveling East.

Though relieved to leave Hitchcock, it was hard to say good-bye to the soft, golden days of California. "I came from California and had been very happy there," Stephen would later tell author Margaret Mitchell.[62] And while Georgia inspired romantic visions of the Civil War, it also triggered fear. For Georgia was a home of the sinister Ku Klux Klan—a secret organization that killed people, especially African-Americans and those who opposed the Klan in any way. In Stephen's mind danced images of black crosses and white-hooded strangers. The images were so strong he included them in a poem before he left Benicia:

> A black cross is set against his name.
> They came to his house in the night.
> The door opens, a rifle shot,
> And the house lies under a blight. [63]

Stephen's fears of the Ku Klux Klan show his sensitivity, even at a young age, to the treatment of African-Americans. Throughout his life, however, he recognized his inability—not being African-American himself—to truly describe the African-American experience. As he says in his most famous poem, *John Brown's Body*:

I cannot sing you, having too white a heart,
And yet, some day, a poet will rise to sing you
And sing you with such truth and mellowness . . .
That you will be a match for any song. [c]

***

Laura had graduated from Vassar College in Poughkeepsie, New York, in 1906 and William from Yale University in New Haven, Connecticut, in 1908. Laura had moved back in with the family, so she traveled East with Stephen, her parents, and Aunt Agnes. William, however, was living on his own in New York City, where he was an editor for *Century Magazine* and would soon, in early September of 1911, marry the middle Thompson sister, Teresa.[64]

In moving to the southern states of America, the Benéts were returning to the area of the country where the family began its American adventure. Back in 1785, just after the end of the American Revolution, a sea captain named Esteban Benét, from the Spanish island of Minorca, brought hungry immigrants to the New World. These new arrivals paid off the cost of their passage by working on the plantation of a Scottish landowner, near the Spanish-settled city of St. Augustine, in what later would become the American state of Florida. When the Territory of Florida became part of the United States, Esteban's son Pedro became the Customs Collector of the Port at St. Augustine. Pedro's son—another Esteban—got the chance to go to the United States Military Academy at West Point. Esteban's English professor at West Point suggested he Americanize his name. The result was the first Stephen Vincent Benét, grandfather to the poet. The Benét family stayed in Florida until the outbreak of the Civil War. When Florida joined the Confederacy, West Point graduate Stephen Vincent Benét joined the Union.[65]

The Benét home at the Augusta Arsenal was another pillared mansion. With its stately bearing and cool, high ceilinged rooms, it might have been the manor house on a plantation. From Stephen's bedroom window, he could see and hear the large iron salute gun that was fired each sunrise and sunset.[66] In the new house he felt comfortable. And, since there was no sign of mysterious strangers in white hoods, he began to settle into his new home. As time passed he began to appreciate that he was living in the heart of Civil War country.

Civil War history didn't just surround the house—it often came to visit. At his mother's teas, elderly ladies nodded gray heads, fluttered lace handkerchiefs, and mourned the losses of the "War Between the States" as if they had just happened. To people in 1911, the Civil War had not happened that long ago. Men who had fought, and women who had lost fathers, sons, and brothers still lived.

---

c. African-American Poet Robert Hayden read these words and sought to take up the challenge to write about the Civil War and slavery from the African-American perspective. "Robert Hayden" on "The Writer's Almanac" with Garrison Keillor, August 4, 2002, writersalmanac.publicradio.org/index.php?date=2002/08/04 (accessed August 6, 2015). For more see Hayden discussion in "Part Eight" below.

The house and Arsenal were located in the area of Augusta known as "Summerville." Here many wealthy families had second homes where they could escape the steamy summer heat of downtown, though it was but a few miles away.

Since the family felt the nearby high school, the Summerville Academy, would be sufficiently challenging, Stephen was enrolled that fall. His classmates were boys and girls living on local plantations or in the small, nearby, middle-class neighborhood. Many of their fathers worked at the Arsenal. Stephen, as the commanding officer's son, got a good share of admiration and respect. In contrast to Hitchcock, where he had felt bullied, here he was welcomed into the baseball games and found eager readers for his poetry.[67]

When the summer heat even in Summerville became too thick, the family, like many others in the South, traveled towards the cool, lush Blue Ridge Mountains of North Carolina.[68] In the mountains Stephen discovered new places and new creatures: birds called "whippoorwills," after the "whip-or-will" cry they made, and mountain fiddlers—men, and the occasional woman, who played an instrument Stephen had always called a violin.

Mountain fiddlers are a unique breed. The rousing music they play—sometimes called "bluegrass"—gets the audience stamping its feet and clapping along. Stephen loved listening to the fiddlers and made a point of following the yearly fiddling contests, which determined the region's top fiddler. [69]

The Benét home at the Augusta Arsenal was another pillared mansion.

Stephen's love of reading remained strong. People spotted him on his bicycle, gliding over the dusty streets of the Arsenal and the town, with an open book wobbling between the handlebars. Entranced by a novel describing some scrappy boy saving the day, or cowboy gunfighters at pistol distance from each other, he was a danger to anyone in his path. He did stop on occasion, when the scene he was reading became just too intense—was the hero about to be captured by the crafty pirates or would he escape?—and he had to read it on firm ground.[70]

In his father's library, Stephen discovered a four-volume work called *American History Told by Contemporaries*.[71] This work broke American history into four categories: "Era of Colonization" (1492-1689), "Building of the Republic" (1689-1783), "National Expansion" (1783-1845), and "Welding of the Nation" (1845-1900). The bulk of the text quoted original documents: a letter from Christopher Columbus; the letters of a young woman visiting New York in the late 1700s, describing the latest fashions for her sister; the diaries, letters and speeches of presidents and generals. For Stephen, the words were not something left behind by people long dead, but, rather, captivating mind-pictures that would stimulate his imagination for the rest of his life. With this book, his love of reading joined with his love of American history, and, though each volume of the work was close to 700 pages, he read the entire thing.

Despite all his reading, Stephen still had time to attend the movies with his father each week. The two even paid extra for the better seats.[72] These were the years of silent movies—adventure and science fiction stories, comedians like the Keystone Kops and Charlie Chaplin.

Another father-and-son activity in the dusty Augusta heat was letter-writing, a pastime that arose out of Stephen's affection for the works of Jack London.

Jack London wrote exciting adventure stories often set in far-away places like the wilds of Alaska, but he also had strong political views. Before earning his living as a writer, Jack had struggled for money, working long, hot hours in a laundry and a fish cannery. In these places Jack watched other workers lose fingers and hands to the machines while earning barely enough money to pay for food and a place to sleep. These experiences led Jack to embrace socialism, a social system in which the community owns the land and businesses. Under capitalism, America's socio-economic system, private individuals own the land and businesses.

For a time, Stephen saw himself as a "Jack London socialist." When the colonel learned of this, he devised a light-hearted way to point out the dangers involved, in his view, should an attempt be made to replace American capitalism with any other social system. The colonel wrote letters to Stephen in red ink, describing violent plots to overthrow America's capitalist system. He signed these letters "Yours for the Revolution." In later life Stephen often wondered—if someone in the War Department had seen one of those letters, written by a U.S Army arsenal commander, what would he have thought?[73]

While in Augusta, Stephen, now fourteen, entered a second *St. Nicholas Magazine* contest with a poem about Robin Hood called "A Song of the Woods." This time Stephen won a "Silver Badge," and his poem was published in the September 1912 issue. The poem describes ghostly visions of Robin Hood and his merry band, visions that just might be visible on the mystical "Midsummer's Eve." Using the same stanza twice, the poem's first and last words are:

> There's many a forest in the world,
> In many lands leaves fall;
> But Sherwood, merry Sherwood,
> Is the fairest wood of all.[74]

Stephen had time to attend the movies every week.

Over the next few years, Stephen continued to win poetry contests—which sometimes came with a cash award—but he'd yet to sell a poem. Finally, in May, 1915, two months before his seventeenth birthday, he had his first sale. The poem was called "Winged Man," a retelling of the Greek story of Icarus, the boy with wax and feather wings who flies too close to the sun. Proudly he wrote to William: "The *New Republic* paid me fifteen (Count'em, FIFTEEN) luscious dollars for Icarus. I feel terribly cocky."[75] With fifteen dollars, Stephen could buy even more fifty-cent novels and penny candy bars than he'd been able to get with the prizes he'd won in the past.

Because he'd skipped eighth grade, Stephen graduated from Summerville that June. His plan was to attend college in the fall. As a child, he'd longed to follow his father and grandfather to West Point. His weak eyes, from the bout with scarlet fever, made that impossible. His second choice was to follow William to Yale.

To get into Yale, however, required that Stephen pass its entrance exams. He'd done well at Summerville, winning prizes in several areas at graduation. But had he learned enough to pass the Yale exams? Summerville may have been more academically challenging than Benicia's public high school—still it was much less challenging than the schools attended by most Yale students.

After Stephen took the exams in June, he wrote his mother, who was visiting her family in Pennsylvania: "Nothing much has happened this week . . . except study. Twelve examinations! Which I probably will not pass. Well, maybe not quite that—but if I passed in Geometry, Algebra or Physics—well, I would be surprised!"[76]

Actually, as he learned in July, he'd failed them all.[77]

At first, Stephen could not believe that the comment he'd made in jest to his mother—"I probably will not pass"—had come true. Beyond that, there was the very real problem of where he would go to college if he could not attend Yale, and how whichever college he did attend would impact his future life. During the 1910s, only a school of the caliber of Yale would give Stephen the knowledge, experiences, and contacts that he would need as a member of the professional middle class.

The colonel was not quite ready to give up a Yale education for his younger son. If Stephen had not passed the required exams, he must take them again. So another blow befell Stephen when he heard that he would not be spending the summer with the family in the cool mountains of North Carolina. Instead, he would spend the hot Georgia summer in Augusta with a tutor, studying six days a week.

Stephen did get Sundays off. So what did he do with that time? Did he celebrate his freedom by spending time outside? No—something else demanded freedom, something else was desperate to live: his poetry. Stephen spent those Sundays writing poems.

Over six weeks he wrote six poems—each the speech of a different man during the fall of the Roman Empire. These poems are remarkable because Stephen—a seventeen-year-old boy—describes, in verse, the pain of aged Roman leaders as each mourns his loss of love, youth, and power.

When Stephen showed his work to William, who had by now published two books of poetry, William formed the poems into a book called *Five Men and Pompey* and found a small publisher in Boston, called Four Seas, to publish it.[78] With this help from William, Stephen experienced his first lesson in the importance of networking.

***

The leaves of the New Haven trees were just beginning to turn gold, orange, and red when Stephen arrived at Yale in the fall of 1915. Though he was the author of a published book, he'd not yet been admitted—he still had to pass those entrance exams.

In his hotel room, waiting to take the exams, Stephen missed his family and could not help but think of his time at Hitchcock. What would Yale be like?

William had enjoyed Yale, as had Stephen's tutor, a young man who had graduated two years before. But "Red" Lewis had often been unhappy at the school. Sometimes, during his visits to Benicia, when Lewis described undergraduate life, it had sounded much like life at Hitchcock.[79]

Stephen shivered, remembering the leering faces of the older boys at Hitchcock, and

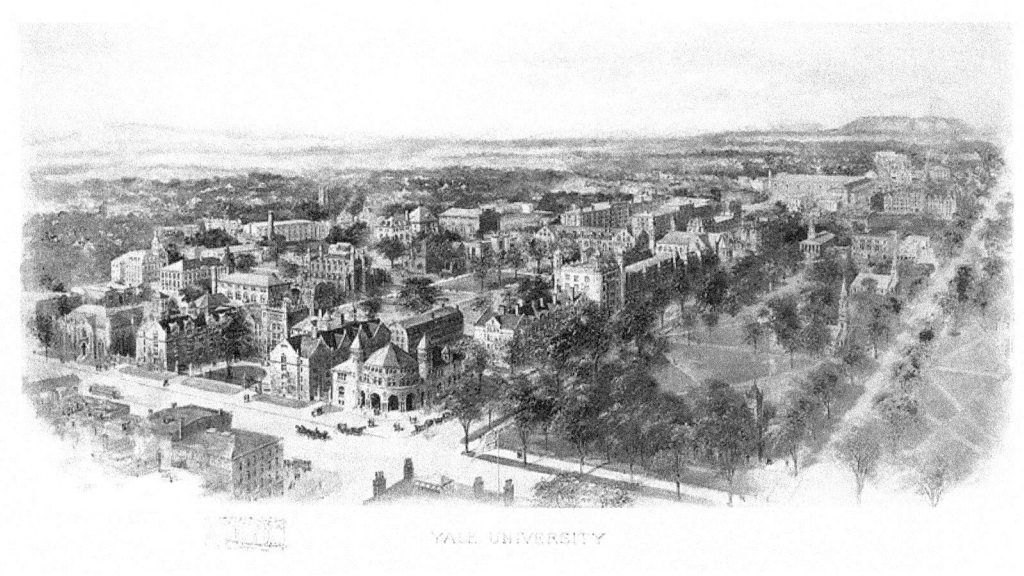

Yale University, circa 1915.

feeling again the twisting of his wrist and arm behind his back while he was derided and laughed at. Was he about to enter the comfortable, chummy atmosphere William had experienced, or another place of pain?

And you may die in the perfumed sheets
But I shall die in battle.

From "The Retort Discourteous"[80]

PART THREE: COLLEGE MAN

Stephen had to pass twelve entrance exams, including algebra, geometry, and physics, the subjects he found most difficult. These exams were not like the SATs of today. A possible algebra question: "Find by logarithms, using arithmetical complements, the value of the following: $[(0.02183)^2 \times (7)^{2/5}] / [\sqrt{(0.0046)} \times 23.309]$"—without, of course, using a calculator. A possible history and geography question: "Leonidas, Pausanias, Lysander."[81] To answer, the test taker would need to know the biographies of Leonidas, a king of the Ancient Greek city-state of Sparta; Pausanias, a Spartan general; and Lysander, a Spartan admiral. Other questions, like those on the entrance exam for Columbia University in 1899, might have required a thorough knowledge of epic poems like *Paradise Lost* by John Milton, Alexander Pope's translation of the *Iliad*, and Samuel Taylor Coleridge's *The Rime of the Ancient Mariner*, as well as novels, a play or two by Shakespeare, a couple of biographies, and some published essays and speeches.[82] Obviously, you would not know in advance which books you might be asked about. Finally, there were often foreign-language exams—depending on the Ivy League school administering the test—including ancient Greek and Latin.

Stephen's summer study paid off: he passed all the exams on his first try. Now that he was an official Yale student, he was able to move out of his hotel and into a dorm.

He was not just an ordinary student at Yale, however—other students were calling him the "Freshman Poet," since he'd published a book of poetry before entering college. The book was short, about fifty pages, and would have reached a limited audience, but it was enough to elevate Stephen to "published author" status.

In addition to *Five Men and Pompey*, he'd written a stack of poems over the summer, and every month he'd send three or four of these to the *Yale Literary Magazine*. His success was impressive: he managed to publish at least one poem each month, with two in February and two—plus a short story—in April. [83]

The first of these published poems was "Three Days' Ride," a melodramatic, romantic tale designed to stir passions,[84] even if Stephen's personal romantic experiences had been limited to the chaste friendships he'd had with girls in high school. In the poem, the daughter of Belton Castle has eloped with her lover. The poem, narrated by the lover, describes the effort of the two to reach, and cross, the Solway River,

Stephen's *Yale Yearbook* photo.

three days' ride from the Castle. The journey is one of sleeplessness and exhaustion for both humans and horses, yet the lovers reach the Solway. Before they can cross, however:

> They came behind us as we kissed,
> Stealthily from the dripping mist,
> Her brothers and their evil band.

The brothers waste no time in killing their sister as her lover watches:

> And she was gone—and a red thing lay
> Silent, on the trampled clay.

But the poem is not over. The narrator describes how he is bound to his horse and led to

> . . . the gallows-tree
> Where I shall hang right speedily, [85]

By his sophomore year, Stephen had moved well beyond the *Yale Literary Magazine*, having published poems in several national magazines.[86] One long poem, "The Drug Shop," is about an old-fashioned drug store filled with jars of various herbal concoctions, the type of shop used by the public before the invention of modern medicines. A shop assistant opens one of the jars and has a drug-inspired dream. In the dream, a genie emerges from one of the jars, offering a choice: the assistant, who is a fisherman in the dream, must sing a brave song or do something the genie cannot do, otherwise he will die. The fisherman/shop assistant sings a glorious song, which brings forth "a gold-robed princess" to whom the fisherman declares his love. Love—that is what the genie cannot do, and so the genie is defeated. [87]

"The Drug Shop" won an important literary prize from Yale, judged by three college professors, including poet Robert Frost of Amherst College and Charles Gayley of the University of California. The prize included publication of the poem as a book. Also containing more of Stephen's poems, the book was called *Young Adventure*. Now, with two books to his credit, as well as his many poems in magazines, he was beginning to become known as a poet beyond Yale. [88]

Despite his literary successes, Stephen did not spend all his time alone with his writing. This was college, and he took advantage of it—dining sometimes with members of the football team, sometimes with literary friends, occasionally with professors.[89] In this way, Stephen was developing contacts and friendships that would be with him—and would often help him with his writing and publishing—for the rest of his life.

As far as finding time to write poetry, Stephen needed no special time for that. He wrote the poetry as it came to him—in class, socializing with friends in the dorms, at crowded restaurant tables. This drove one of his good friends, John Farrar, quite crazy. Every day Farrar locked himself in his room for at least two hours to write poetry, yet Stephen published many more poems than Farrar did. Though Stephen's ease with poetry may have frustrated Farrar in college, their friendship would benefit both in the future. Eventually, Farrar gave up poetry to focus on running a publishing company. That company, Farrar & Rinehart—later, Farrar, Straus and Giroux—would become Stephen's primary publisher.[90] In turn, Stephen would become one of Farrar's bestselling authors.

***

Back in 1914, the year before Stephen entered Yale, war had erupted in Europe. Germany had used the excuse of the assassination of an Austrian archduke and his wife to attempt to create a great German Empire encompassing Belgium, France, Great Britain, and a good chunk of Russia.⁹¹ Almost immediately, the Allied countries—Great Britain, Russia, and France—were fighting the Central Powers—Germany and Austria-Hungary. By early 1917, the Allies were struggling, and it had become clear that America must join the Allies to prevent their possible defeat.

America's entry into what was now being called "the Great War"—later called "World War I"—meant that, by April 1917, Stephen's carefree college days were over. Suddenly, attending classes seemed frivolous and unnecessary as college students across America raced each other to enlist in the Army or the Navy.

Stephen's only thought at this time was to join his classmates heading to Europe. Persistently, stubbornly, he trekked from recruiter to recruiter. All, however, rejected him because of his weak eyes. For the same reason, those eyes had dashed his dream of West Point. Now they kept him from any military service.⁹²

Yale sought to make the students left behind feel that they, too, were in the fight. One way they did this was by bringing in drillmasters to march groups around the Quad. One drillmaster was a young major in the Canadian Army recovering from shell shock after serving on the Western Front. His name was Raymond Massey. Later he would become a famous Hollywood actor who would be nominated for an Oscar in 1940 for his role as Abraham Lincoln. Massey would also become a frequent performer of the works of Stephen Vincent Benét on both radio and the stage.⁹³

Marching about awkwardly in the safety of Yale only made Stephen feel silly and more powerless than he already felt. And then he began hearing about the deaths: one fellow he'd often chatted with in the library, dead in a training accident; others whose names and faces he knew, felled by the flu; and then the combat deaths.

All Stephen could do was turn to his poetry. "For God, for country, for Yale!' is the cry / Of men who have left us, to conquer or die," he wrote, repeating the words used to urge young men to join the American Army and head for Europe. Yet if the Army had rejected you, as it had Stephen, the words one then heard were: "*Study your English—you'll help win the war!*" (italics in original).⁹⁴ This was not enough for Stephen. Feeling the call to serve in battle, he could not accept that remaining behind to study would help win the war in any way.

His frustration grew. He could not continue to sit idly by while others were dying for him. There must be a way he could leave English class behind. Then he had an idea: he memorized the eye chart before presenting himself to the Army once again.

This time, he was in. Almost immediately he was sent to a New Jersey camp, and given his first assignment: Kitchen Patrol, or KP. Unfortunately, while he was peeling potatoes, the sergeant-in-charge walked by. After watching Stephen for a while, the sergeant became concerned that Stephen was carving the potatoes so close to his nose he might cut it off. This led to a second eye test with a different chart, and Stephen's discharge.⁹⁵

By August 1918, Stephen had managed to obtain a job as an office clerk in the State Department in Washington, D.C. At least this job brought him closer to the action than Yale. Being in Washington also brought him into contact with other writers, including his brother William, who was stationed in Washington as a ground officer in the Air Corps (which would become the Air

Force many years later.) In October Stephen was transferred to a job he might have liked better than clerical work—he became a cryptographer with Military Intelligence. In this job Stephen assisted with the breaking of enemy messages written in code.

Ultimately, Stephen's view of war work in Washington was harsh. In later years, he described many of the men he saw there as: "the wranglers, and the schemers, the men who burrow and strive and breed like blow-flies in the vast intricate web of army organization behind the front line." Stephen's work in Washington ended on December 21, 1918, six weeks after the end of the war.[96]

Returning to Yale with the veterans, it seemed to Stephen that everyone possessed a new eagerness for study. The time away from Yale, the turbulence of war experiences, time spent on mind-numbing office work—whatever the reason, the war seemed to have given Stephen and his classmates a new appreciation for knowledge.

While Stephen had been in Washington, Yale University Press had published his second book, the collection of poems entitled *Young Adventure*, a book to which, he was pleased to learn, the critics gave "generous and enthusiastic" praise.[97]

With two published books and poems in numerous magazines, it seemed that Stephen's choice of career was clear—he would make his living as a poet and writer. The only problem with this plan was that all that he had published over the past four years had earned so little money it wasn't even enough to live on for six months.[98] At the time, women did not often work outside the home and, even if they did work, they usually earned much less than men performing similar jobs. Therefore, beyond the need to earn his own living expenses, if Stephen wanted a wife and a family, very likely he would have to earn all the family income.

By mid-1919, with graduation approaching, he considered graduate school, even though his post-war eagerness for study was fading and he'd grown weary of books and professors. Then he began hearing that some other young writers were finding a decent income in a new field called advertising. One of these was named F. Scott Fitzgerald. While Stephen was contributing to the *Yale Literary Magazine*, Fitzgerald had been a student at Princeton writing for that school's literary magazine. Fitzgerald would one day write *The Great Gatsby* and other books about rich young people in and around New York City in the early twentieth century. In 1919, he'd taken work at a New York ad agency, thinking that such work would pay him for writing, as well as show the young woman he wished to marry that he could support her. Given his similar goals, Stephen thought, why not give ad-writing a try?[99]

Soon Stephen was working in a vast room of writers and secretaries in the New York City offices of Charles W. Hoyt, Planned Advertising. From the beginning, ad agency copy writing meant toiling eight hours a day to come up with phrases to make people eager to buy soap and underwear. The work was so unpleasant for Stephen that he could only do it for three months.[100] Office work itself might have been something Stephen was not cut out for. Before he left the ad agency, he wrote a few poems about it. These lines are from "Lunch Time Along Broadway":

> Twelve-thirty bells from a thousand clocks, the type-
>   writer tacks and stops,

> Gorged elevators slam and fall through the floors like
> water-drops,
> From offices hung like sea-gulls' nests on a cliff the whirl-
> winds beat,
> The octopus-crowd comes rolling out, his tentacles crawl
> for meat.[101]

"Lunch Time on Broadway" describes office workers as if they were part of a giant, sinister factory—sinister, because the output of the poem's office tower is a huge, ravenous octopus crawling through the streets of New York in search of lunch every workday at 12:30 p.m.

The poem does more than merely create the visual image of an octopus. It seems to offer Stephen's view of office life in New York City: the individual lost among towers filled with workers doing similar, repetitive actions. Stephen was even more specific about his feelings for office work when, later in his life, he said that a job in an office "is my idea of hell without grandeur. I would rather be kept in a cage."[102]

From his three months in advertising, Stephen had earned some money. The time away from Yale had made him ready—in fact, eager—to return to books and professors. In the fall of 1919, he applied for the Masters of Arts program in English at Yale and, even though the school year had already begun, was awarded a fellowship that would provide him with money on which he could live while he studied.[103]

The postcard above shows popular tourist attractions in New York City in the early Twentieth Century, including the Statue of Liberty, the Brooklyn Bridge, the Flatiron Building, and Grant's Tomb.

Though a Yale M.A. was supposed to take two years, Stephen had a third book of poetry ready to publish by the end of his first year, and he was allowed to submit that book as his thesis.[104] On June 16, 1920, he received his Masters of Arts degree, and was awarded an even larger fellowship for the 1920-21 school year. This new fellowship was particularly attractive because it allowed him to study at other schools besides Yale, including schools in Europe. If he could manage to earn just a bit more money to supplement the fellowship, he could study in a city he'd long dreamed about: Paris, France.[105]

The apple has a Springtime smell,
The star-fields silver grain,
But I have youth, the cockleshell,
And the sweet laugh of Jane.

From "Dulce Ridentem"[106]

PART FOUR: POET IN LOVE

Back in March 1919, with Stephen soon to graduate from college, his father was transferred from the arsenal in Augusta back to the arsenal in Watervliet, New York.[107] Though the colonel had left Watervliet back in 1905 as a major, he was retuning as a colonel *and* the officer in charge.

In June of 1920, his Masters of Arts degree completed, Stephen headed to Watervliet, where his family had again settled. There, in the commanding officer's quarters, he would work on getting that extra money he needed to travel to Paris in the fall.

The Watervliet house, shaded by trees and surrounded by emerald lawn, was spacious and easily held the family, which still included Aunt Agnes, but now also William and his children. Sadly, in January 1919, William's wife Teresa had died during a flu epidemic that swept the world. At Watervliet, William had his mother and sister to help with six-year-old James, five-year-old Rosemary—called Penny—and three-year-old Kathleen—called Kit.[108]

At first, the money Stephen needed came quickly: a member of the Yale faculty loaned him $500. Now if he could just finish the novel he was working on, called *The Beginning of Wisdom*, then sell it to a publisher, he'd have all the money he'd need.

The Beginning of Wisdom is the story of a young man who grows up in California in a Benicia-like town,[109] enjoys writing poetry, goes to Yale, and struggles for "personal liberation." About this book, Stephen said later: "The first novel I ever wrote . . . was on the struggles and soul-strivings of a very young man. And parts of it are perfectly appalling, [though] . . . I did take him over a lot of jumps."[110]

By mid-August, Stephen had written enough of the book to submit it to the publisher Henry Holt and hope for an advance—money that would be paid before the book was published, in "advance" of the book earning royalties. The school year was about to begin, and Stephen couldn't wait any longer. On August 28, with what money he already had, Stephen boarded an ocean-liner for France, hoping the advance would eventually follow him.[111]

His plans for the following year were vague. Rather than studying at Yale, he was to be studying at the Sorbonne University in Paris. Yet, as his father explained to a family friend: "Yale gave [Stephen] a traveling fellowship and he is supposed to be studying at the Sorbonne . . . Studying what I don't know. Just studying I imagine."[112]

Actually Stephen was at the Sorbonne very seldom. Upon first arriving in Paris, he moved in with his Uncle Laurence Benét—a wealthy official for Hotchkiss et Cie, an international weapons maker. Laurence is credited with inventing the Hotchkiss machine gun, the standard machine gun used by the French and the Americans during the First World War and therefore essential in the defeat of Germany. Interestingly, Laurence also founded the American Ambulance Service, which transported wounded soldiers from battlefronts to hospitals during the First World War.[113]

Laurence and his wife Margaret were well liked by both French and Americans, who saw the Benét home as a second American Embassy.[114]

Two views of the Commanding Officer's Quarters at Watervliet

At Uncle Larry's, Stephen finished *The Beginning of Wisdom*. Almost as soon as it was sent to the publisher Henry Holt, another book of his poems was published, this one entitled *Heaven and Earth*. Though this was his fourth book of poetry, it was the first to be accepted by a major New York publisher, Holt and Company, which published poets like Carl Sandburg and Robert Frost, great poets whom Stephen was pleased to join.[115]

With his novel done, Stephen settled in to enjoy Paris life. He took an apartment with two friends and began touring the bars and nightclubs. The bar of the fancy Ritz Hotel, for example, was a favorite hangout. His apartment became a popular gathering place for visiting Americans, like the poet Edna St. Vincent Millay. And Stephen continued to attend parties and dinners for the rich and fashionable of Paris at Uncle Larry's.[116]

Support for Stephen's Paris lifestyle came with the news that publisher Holt had accepted *The Beginning of Wisdom*. The long-awaited advance soon followed.

Back home in New York, there was some discontent. In her correspondence with her son, Mrs. Benét complained that his letters were too brief. In contrast, his father assured him that his mother was overreacting, and would be happy only if she were to receive a detailed history of Stephen's whole day from the time he put on his underwear. His father added: "We are waiting anxiously . . . for your scraps from the Sorbonne and [a report, entitled] "The Sorbonne: what it is, why Young Americans Like it and What They Do There."[117]

Then Stephen met *her,* in late November 1920, at the apartment of friends. Her name was Rosemary Carr. A friend, according to one of Stephen's biographers, called her "gay and grave, tender and remote."[118] One of the most charming descriptions of her is from William, when he describes his first meeting with her in an autobiographical poem. After noting her amused smile he remarks that she is "affectionate and shy," with "clear blue eyes and roseleaf skin," a "straight slimness," and a "little quirk of laughter at the corner of mouth and eyes."[119]

The Beginning of Wisdom, Stephen's first novel

From the moment they met, and for the rest of their lives together, Stephen wrote poems about her. From the adoring:

> You are the soul, enchanted with its wings,
> The single voice that raises up the dead
> To shake the pride of angels.[120]

To the humorous:

> Oh when you are with me, my heart is white steel
> But the bat's in the belfry, the mold's in the meal,
> And I think I hear skeletons climbing the stair!
> —Rosemary, Rosemary, let down your bright hair![121]

They also read poems by other poets together. One favorite was a short poem called "Bunches of Grapes" by Walter de la Mare:

> "Bunches of grapes," says Timothy;
> "Pomegranates pink," says Elaine;
> "A junket of cream and a cranberry tart
>   For me," says Jane.
>
> . . .
>
> "Chariots of gold," says Timothy;
> "Silvery wings," says Elaine;
> "A bumpity ride in a wagon of hay
>   For me," says Jane

Because of de la Mare's poem, Stephen began calling Rosemary "Jane."[122]

Rosemary was a recent graduate of the University of Chicago. Her grades had been so good that she'd been accepted into the prestigious honor society, Phi Beta Kappa—an achievement Stephen could not claim. She was one of only a few American women reporters working in Paris at the time, writing fashion stories and features for the *Chicago Tribune* and the *London Daily Mail*.

After meeting Rosemary, Stephen no longer had time for bars and nightclubs. By early 1921, he'd begun writing again, completing four short stories and six poems in one month.[123]

Apparently, he intrigued Rosemary as well. The day after meeting him, she wrote her mother: He's a "poet, [a] real genius, it seems. You should see him! . . . [B]ites his fingernails, but is too smart for words." Later, she sent her mother "Steve's poems about me," explaining: "Steve simply writes poetry about what is nearest to him—and we have seen a lot of each other this winter."[124]

The two became engaged on March 17, 1921—sharing a kiss on a dark Paris back street, outside a bar, an Italian restaurant, or a printing plant—Stephen could not remember which. He even returned to the approximate spot and "stood there in the rain this morning like a fool trying to decide which it was." Deciding to ask Rosemary which she'd prefer, he told her—"all might be symbolic except the Italian restaurant. I don't know what that would stand for."[125]

In June 1921 Stephen's school year in Paris was over. In the same month, leaving the sun glistening on the Seine River, he returned to America. According to their plan, Rosemary left Paris as well—though she took a later boat to prevent questions from her family.

Rosemary's boss at the *Chicago Tribune* hated to see her go, insisting on giving her a letter of recommendation highly praising her work and abilities. He hoped she might one day return full-time to the newspaper field, but she never did.[126]

By the time Stephen headed back to America he'd begun a second novel, *Jean Huguenot*, the story of a beautiful but unhappy southern belle. He was counting on this book to earn enough money to pay for a wedding and a Paris honeymoon.[127]

Arriving in New York, he found his parents living in a very different home from the spacious Watervleit commanding officer's quarters he'd left the year before. Due to retire in July 1921, the colonel had hoped to move to "the South Seas or California or some place with a desert climate," as he told a friend. Instead, he was in Scarsdale, New York, in a small house that could barely hold him plus wife, daughter, Aunt Agnes (now eighty-seven), son William, and William's three children. After Stephen arrived, the family nicknamed the house "the Brimming Cup."[128]

"Our present mode of living . . . is intimate to say the least," Stephen wrote to Rosemary. "We are crowded into the house. . . and have no servants. Consequently I dry dishes, split kindling etc. etc."[129]

Stephen and Rosemary around the time of their engagement.

By this time William was working as an associate editor at the *Literary Review of The New York Evening Post* and spending evenings and weekends sitting at the dining-room table writing a novel called *First Person Singular*,[130] which would be published in 1922.[131] Mrs. Benét was busy with housework and caring for her three grandchildren.[132] Laura had just spent four years as a social worker at the Spring Street Settlement House in Manhattan. With the need now to help care for William's children she turned to writing, work she could do at home. During this time she worked as a book reviewer and an editorial assistant for two New York newspapers.[133] The colonel planned "to write my memoirs in seventeen volumes . . . and generally do as I please if my family will allow me."[134] Still, even he helped out around the house. "Father is magnificent," Stephen wrote Rosemary, he looked just like a great, ancient general "running a vacuum cleaner."[135]

Since William had commandeered the dining room table, and with all the comings and goings, there was no place in the house for Stephen to write, so he found a spot for himself in the garage. Though the space was pretty hot, beneath a tin roof, and the smell of gasoline constantly made him sneeze, he dutifully continued working on *Jean Huguenot*. No hardship could stop him; finishing the book meant marriage to Rosemary.

While Stephen labored in that hot garage in Scarsdale, Rosemary was in Chicago. When she'd docked in New York, her mother had met her and the two stopped to meet the Benét family on their way to Chicago. During that visit, Stephen and Rosemary were never out of the sight of Mrs. Carr, a medical doctor, who was used to being in charge and having her orders followed.[136]

Stephen spent his time in that hot garage with a typewriter like this one.

As soon as *Jean Hugenot* was finished, Stephen hoped to make a quick sale—and then it would be wedding-planning time. Several of his friends had recently sold work to *Harper's Bazaar* magazine and suggested he try to sell his book there. The magazine would then serialize the book, publishing a portion of it in each issue. By publishing first in a magazine, a writer could earn money for the serial rights to his work, as well as more income later when the book was published as a single volume.

In the 1920s, with a little effort, a writer could often obtain a meeting with a magazine's editor, and Stephen managed to obtain a meeting with Harry Sell, the editor of *Harper's Bazaar*. The two met in Sell's "shiny expensive office." Sell was interested; he thought the book might work well as a serial and he promised to read the manuscript over the weekend. [137]

Yet, after reading *Jean Hugenot*, Sell decided against it—and Stephen was in despair.[138] Now he must try again to find a purchaser for his book before he could marry Rosemary. And it didn't help that he was feeling distant from her, feeling as if she might "vanish forever into some Midwestern void."[139]

Glumly, he returned to his typewriter, struggling both to write and to sell what he wrote. One day his Yale friend John Farrar arranged a meeting for him with a literary agent named Carl Brandt. An agent could sell Stephen's work while Stephen focused on writing.[140]

For Stephen, the meeting with Brandt was a momentous event. The two liked each other immediately, and that first meeting began a close, lifelong relationship. Stephen's first description of Brandt, included in a letter to Rosemary, doesn't quite suggest the importance Brandt would have in Stephen's life. As Stephen said, the agent was "a very nice blond fat person looking somewhat like a plump blond sea lion with a soft and pleasing voice."[141]

With Brandt, Stephen could talk freely about all his economic concerns. His first concern, of course, was his need for money immediately, so that he might marry Rosemary. A close second was his need to know if he could make a living as a writer—with a wife.

The way to earn the most money, Brandt explained, leaning back in his large desk chair, was to write serials rather than short stories. And then he gave Stephen some pointers on how to write a popular serial: be sure the tale has a chase scene in it. Oh, and "whatever you do, *don't get your hero and heroine into bed before the final installment* . . . If you do, you'll lose a hundred percent of your women readers and a hundred and five percent of the men" (emphasis added).[142]

Soon after meeting Brandt, Stephen began a serial that would become his third novel: *Young People's Pride*. In this tale of youthful friendships and romance and the emotions thus stirred, he poured out his feelings for the absent Rosemary, particularly as he watched friends falling in love, getting married, spending time together. [143]

Despite Brandt's advice, Stephen still wrote short stories. He could write these more quickly than a serial or a novel, and each one he sold brought in sorely needed money. Over time, however, it became hard for Stephen to write the types of short stories that were the most likely to sell, growing weary of trying to figure out how to get his hero or heroine free of the evil villains each story must have.[144]

Finally, in October, 1921, money started to trickle in. First, Henry Sell at *Harper's Bazaar* paid him $250 (more than $3,000 in today's dollars)[d] for having held on to *The Beginning of Wisdom* for several weeks, even though Sell had decided not to publish it as a serial. Next, the Poetry Society announced it would split the

Harper's Bazaar cover for August, 1920.

---

d. Throughout the text, current dollars as of 2015 have been calculated using the "CPI Inflation Calculator" of the U.S. Department of Labor, Bureau of Labor Statistics, http://www.bls.gov/data/inflation_calculator.htm accessed September 2015.

year's prize for best volume of poetry between Stephen's *Heaven and Earth* and Carl Sandburg's *Smoke and Steel.* Stephen's share was $250. Third, Henry Sell decided to buy *Young People's Pride* and use it as a five-part serial. And fourth, Brandt called—twice—each time to report the sale of a short story.

"Money collected today," he informed Rosemary on October 19. "Make plans accordingly. I love you darling."[145]

After the struggle to earn enough money, and the months they'd been apart, Stephen and Rosemary were going to marry and then return to Paris, the city in which they'd met and where they'd been so happy. They were "going back . . . sink or swim, live or die, survive or perish!"[146]

Stephen Vincent Benét and Rosemary Carr were married near her home in Chicago on November 26, 1921. A few days later, they sailed for Paris. With them was a check for $1,794.10 (just under $22,000 in today's dollars), which was all—"the final, net, five star sum" they possessed.[147]

Go play with the towns you have built of blocks
The towns where you would have bound me!
I sleep in my earth like a tired fox,
 And my buffalo have found me.

From "The Ballad of William Sycamore"[148]

PART FIVE: STRUGGLING WRITER

The money Stephen had earned financed a three-month honeymoon that took the newlyweds from Paris to the Italian Riviera. By February, though, Agent Brandt was sending stern cablegrams urging Stephen to get back to New York. Now was Stephen's time to break into the writing profession, and the place to do that was New York City.

Stephen was not eager to return to New York, because there he'd be unable to avoid the "New York literary" scene. New York literary people, to Stephen, were a special type that he didn't like. Among them, except for the few he counted as friends, he saw "back biting and posing and [a] general nervous hurried air of going somewhere faster than anybody else" reminding him of "jumping educated fleas."[149]

Eventually, in the late spring of 1922, Stephen and Rosemary did return to the United States. Almost immediately Stephen had the satisfaction of watching his short stories appear in a variety of popular magazines like *Cosmopolitan, Redbook* and *The Ladies' Home Journal*. At this rate of success, if Stephen kept writing short stories, Brandt estimated he could earn $5,000 to $7,500 in a year, (in today's money that would be earnings in the $71,000 to $106,000 range). [150]

***

Covers from *Cosmopolitan Magazine* and *The Ladies' Home Journal* from the early 1920s.

It's important to remember—even if it may be hard to imagine—that during the early 1920s there were no televisions, computers, iPods, tablets or smartphones, let alone videos, DVDs, computer games, or Internet.

Movies were silent, and radio programming was still developing. Even in a live theater, if you had one near your home, there was a limited supply of situation comedies and light-hearted romances. Magazine short stories helped fill people's need for entertainment.

There was a small problem with Stephen's short-story success, however. Even though he'd returned refreshed from his three months in Europe, and despite the fun of seeing many of his short stories in print, he still disliked writing the types of stories he could sell. "This damn man in my story is strapped on an operating table," he told Rosemary. "I must leap and either save or kill him. I'd much prefer [to kill him], but I'm afraid he's worth more money living than dead."[151]

Early on, Stephen earned around $125 to $200 per story.[152] As he mastered the stereotype editors wanted—that is, as he began writing stories where lovers meet and the tale ends happily—he was earning as much as $500 per story by 1924, or almost $7,000 in today's money.[153]

In addition to an income, his short stories were also bringing him a touch of fame. One story blurb described him as "an author whom people are talking a lot about these days."[154]

But the poetry would not be silenced. Despite the money the short stories could bring in, still he needed to write the poetry. Something else was finding release in the poetry now as well: Stephen's great love for America. "The Ballad of William Sycamore," one of his first post-college poetry successes, exudes his love of American history.[155]

William Sycamore represents the American pioneer—born in a log cabin, he follows the wagons west and sows "his sons like apple-seed." One son dies at the Alamo and another falls with Custer, deaths he accepts as part of the reality of life. But when it comes to watching his land fenced and towns begin to grow, he is broken. [156]

In 1948, the *Literary History of the United States* called "The Ballad of William Sycamore" the "incarnation of [America's] pioneer spirit."[157] Later the singer Steve Young would sing the ballad on his album *Solo/Live* and in a YouTube clip.[158]

For the rest of Stephen's life, poetry—combined with his love of America and her history—would produce some of his greatest work.

Each poem Stephen wrote seemed to take him deeper into the hearts of his audience. Part of the reason for this was that he liked to write about everyday people in various parts of the country, at various times in America's history. But another reason was that, though Stephen now had a master's degree from an Ivy League school, he wrote for the mass of Americans—most of whom had no more than, at most, a high school education. Readers could understand Stephen's poems immediately, absorbing his message as they read.

And then, of course, each of Stephen's poems directs his reader as a conductor rules his orchestra: here is the place to laugh, here to grieve, now some tears—but then, perhaps, impassioned anger at an injustice, or a cold chill of fear.

In 1924, Stephen's brother William was also living and working in New York. The year before, William had remarried. This time his wife was Elinor Wylie, a twice-divorced woman famous for both her exceptional beauty and her "melodious, sensuous poetry."[159] Professionally, William had just helped to found the *Saturday Review of Literature*, which he would edit until his death in 1950. The *Saturday Review* published poetry as well as play and book reviews. Stephen would be a frequent contributor, as would poet and former Benicia visitor Leonard Bacon.[160]

John Farrar—Stephen's college pal, occasional co-author, frequent publisher and lifelong friend.

In the spring of 1924, Stephen decided to partner with his Yale friend John Farrar and venture into a new literary avenue—play writing. This effort was not as successful as he might have wished. While waiting to hear from a Broadway producer, Stephen wrote a friend that there might be plans for his play "to be put on in the Hippodrome [Theater] with a chorus of diving elephants . . . or it may be in [producer] Lee Shubert's wastebasket. I can't find out."[161]

He did manage to get two of his plays produced in 1924. Both drew on history. The first, *That Awful Mrs. Eaton*, was about Peggy Eaton, the second wife of President Andrew Jackson's Secretary of War. In the play, as in history, the wives of the other cabinet members did not like Mrs. Eaton, seeing her as low class (the daughter of hotel owners!) and a catty flirt. In attempting to help Peggy, Jackson rearranged his cabinet, an act later referred to as "The Petticoat Affair." Some historians believe that Floride Calhoun's hostility to Peggy may have hurt the political fortunes of her husband, Vice President John C. Calhoun. In contrast, Secretary of State Martin Van Buren, a widower, graciously accepted Mrs. Eaton—a fact some believe may have helped Van Buren to later reach the presidency.[162]

The second play, called *Nerves*, was about an aviator experiencing anxiety during the recent World War, which would later be known as World War I.

In the fall of 1924, before the two plays opened, the colonel sent Stephen an update on the thoughts of Mrs. Benét: "Your mother . . . hopes you have got some new clothes and when she comes to New York [for the plays] she wants you to display them."[163]

Unfortunately, both plays did poorly. *Mrs. Eaton*, became—as Stephen phrased it—"that awful, awful *The Awful Mrs. Eaton*."[164] *Nerves* opened three days before *What Price Glory?*—a much better play, even in Stephen's opinion—also about World War I.[165]

Nerves, however, was a turning point in the career of a minor cast member, a young actor named Humphrey Bogart. Surprisingly, Bogart's performance impressed the famous theater critic Alexander Woollcott. Woollcott had so thoroughly trashed Bogart's work in a play two seasons earlier that he was surprised to see the young man still acting. Now the chagrined critic wrote: "Those words are hereby eaten."[166] Bogart would go on to become a famous, Oscar-winning actor in the 1940s and 1950s.

With no money coming in from the plays, and because they'd taken up much of his short-story writing time for many months, Stephen was soon short of funds. Near the end of 1924, his bank account was down to $35.[167]

Something wonderful had happened in 1924, however: on April 6, daughter Stephanie Jane was born. The "Stephanie" was for Stephen, while "Jane" was his nickname for Rosemary.[168]

Now those few dollars in the bank would need to stretch to feed another mouth.

> *It always seemed to me . . . that legends and yarns and*
> *folk-tales are as much a part of the real history of a country*
> *as proclamations and provisions and constitutional amendments.* [169]

PART SIX: WHIPPOORWILL

One day a college dean was to meet Stephen at the railroad station, then take him to the hall where he was to give a lecture. She was nervous; she'd never seen Stephen before and was unsure how she'd recognize him.

"I will wear glasses and probably a brown suit," he told her. "I am not quite sure what I look like . . . but I have several times been taken for an insurance salesman." [170]

An outside observer might also have mentioned Stephen's trim mustache, which he'd grown to rid himself of the "beardless-wonder look."[171] He had been described as "boyish . . . and shy,"[172] a "sparkling conversationalist," a good listener,[173] and "a kind, gentle, understanding person."[174] One publisher even said: "if I had a chance to be some other person whom I had known in my lifetime, I would prefer to have been Stephen Benét, not anyone else."[175]

At public appearances (or "lecture-readings," as he called them) Stephen might—at first—look ill at ease, weary, and nervous, wearing a rumpled suit. Yet when he spoke, it was with a "voice of great power," communicating sincerity, intelligence, and even spiritual energy. When he read his poetry, he tipped back his head and the words poured forth, as one listener commented, with a volume surprising in so gentle a man.[176]

In early 1925, despite his need for money, he managed to write a few more poems. One of these was called "The Mountain Whippoorwill: or How Hill-Billy Jim Won the Great Fiddler's Prize." The poem drew on his memories of teenage summers in the North Carolina mountains, but also on a magazine article he'd read about the 1924 Atlanta Fiddlers' Convention. At that event, a young man named Lewis Stokes beat Fiddlin' John Carson, the elder statesman of fiddlers at that time.[177]

Luckily for Stephen's bank account this poem was immensely popular. On at least one occasion, he was greeted at a party as "Mr. Whippoorwill."[178]

The poem tells the story of Hill-Billy Jim who lives without siblings, parents, pets—or a "whole pair of pants." Jim does have his fiddle—his "little whippoorwill"—and when he plays it "yuh got to start to dance!"

One day Jim takes his fiddle to the Essex County Fair. His goal is first prize in the famous "Fiddler's Show." Of course, nobody expects Hill-Billy Jim to win. And the other fiddlers are good. When old Dan Wheeling was finished, for example, "the crowd cut loose." While poor Jim wondered, "What's the use?"

Yet Jim stood up and took his bow:

> An' my fiddle went to my shoulder, so.
> . . .
> They've fiddled the rose, an' they've fiddled the thorn,
> But they haven't fiddled the mountain-corn.
>
> . . .
> [When he'd finished] They wasn't a sound . . .
> An' I thought, "I've fiddled all night an' lost.
> Yo're a good hill-billy, but yuh've been bossed."
>
> So I went to congratulate old man Dan,
> —But he put his fiddle into my han'—
> An' then the noise of the crowd began. [179]

Years later, the Nitty Gritty Dirt Band recorded the poem as a song—"The Mountain Whippoorwill (Or, How Hillbilly Jim Won the Great Fiddler's Prize)"—featured on their album *Stars & Stripes Forever*.[180] Shortly after that, singer/songwriter Charlie Daniels wrote the song "The Devil Went Down to Georgia"—because he remembered reading "The Mountain Whippoorwill" in high school. Daniels' song was a number-one hit on the country charts, but also crossed over onto the pop charts. The album on which it was released went multi-platinum. In 1979, the song won a Grammy, and in 1980 appeared in the movie *Urban Cowboy*. Later the song appeared in the video game *Guitar Hero III*.[181]

In the mid 1960s, comedian Steve Martin found "Whippoorwill" useful. Needing to expand his first attempt at doing a long act before paying customers, Martin took to reading aloud poetry by e e cummings, T.S. Eliot, Carl Sandburg—and Stephen Vincent Benét. As Martin explained in his book *Born Standing Up: A Comic's Life*: "Nobody cared about hearing Eliot and cummings in a nightclub, but the Benét piece, a socko narrative poem about a fiddle contest in Georgia, stayed in the act for at least a year."[182]

"The Mountain Whippoorwill," together with some of the other poems Stephen had written in the early 1920s, were gathered into a slim volume called *Tiger Joy*.[183] This was Stephen's first book of poetry in several years.

By the time *Tiger Joy* reached bookstores, Stephen was "sweating over a costume-book" to be called *Spanish Bayonet*. By "costume-book" he meant a historical novel, but one with well-developed characters rather than "the stuffed personages of history." To write the book, he put himself on a schedule of 10,000 words per week, which was difficult because, as he told Rosemary, "I have to think till all the wheels go around before I can visualize people in wigs and purple panties."[184]

Though the word "Spanish" appears in the title, this book would be another example of Stephen's love of America. It is set in Spanish-settled eighteenth-century Florida.[185]

The magazine *Pictorial Review* was ready to pay him the huge sum of $10,000 in 1925—more than $136,000 in today's dollars—money he and his family truly needed—to serialize *Spanish Bayonet*. But there was a catch. The magazine wanted the book to end with a wedding. This meant, rather than having the heroine die as Stephen wanted, or even left awaiting the hero's return from war, to which he was willing to agree for $10,000, the hero and heroine had to marry.

Because he could so use the money, and because Brandt assured him that the original ending would be in the book version of the story, Stephen made a great effort to please the magazine. He even went off to a special writer's colony in New England to focus on the story.

Yet Stephen saw that, with each draft allowing the heroine to survive, the book became weaker as it turned into something trite and clichéd. Therefore, in the end, there was no wedding, the heroine stayed dead, and Stephen let *Pictorial Review* keep its $10,000.[186]

Failing to earn that offered money meant economic hardship for his family. Because Stephen had been working on *Spanish Bayonet* rather than money-earning short stories, the family's only income came from Rosemary's earnings from a part-time job at *Vogue* Magazine, and most of that went to pay for the babysitter watching little Stephanie.

After five years of writing with much critical success, Stephen was little better off financially than when he'd begun his writing career. After buying train tickets to send Rosemary and Stephanie to visit her parents in Chicago for a while (which would also save the family some money), he had only five dollars left in the world.[187]

And he had another concern. In a few months, he would have not only a wife and daughter to support—but another child as well.[188]

While working on *Spanish Bayonet*, an idea had begun to dance about in Stephen's head—"a swell idea for a long poem"—a historical poem. The only trouble was it would take him a long time to write, and he'd "have to read an entire library first."[189] Since he barely had enough money to feed his family, he certainly could not finance a large stretch of time for researching and writing. If he could get some financial help, though, he might be able to tackle such an undertaking.

There were organizations like the Guggenheim Memorial Foundation that could provide support, but obtaining a grant from such a foundation would not be easy. Competition was tough. Still, he submitted an application in December of 1925 for a $2500 grant—a comfortable sum, about $34,000 in today's dollars—explaining that he was sick of writing short stories and that he wanted to write a long poem on some American subject. At the time, he had several ideas—including something about the Civil War.[190]

In seeking a letter of recommendation from the Dean at Yale, Stephen expressed his desire for the grant in economic terms: should he get the grant he would be able to write "verse which has no market value, instead of writing what the magazines want, which unfortunately, boils the pot."[191]

It was now early 1926. Needing money, Stephen wrote reviews and articles for various magazines, including an article entitled "My Favorite Fictional Character," which for him was Dr. Watson of the Sherlock Holmes detective stories. With Dr. Watson, Stephen felt comfortable, as if the good doctor were a "solemn, ponderous St. Bernard," with tail wagging.[192]

He also wrote more of the dreaded short stories. But because he was so weary of writing light-hearted romances involving shallow young people, those he did manage to scratch out weren't selling. When he told his agent, Brandt, that he wanted to write a different type of short story, Brandt was ready to support the idea; after all, whatever Stephen might write, it couldn't sell worse than his current stories.[193]

Stephen's new stories were of a higher, more literary quality and drew on his love of history and folk tales.[194] "The Sobbin' Women," for example, tells the tale of seven backwoods brothers in desperate need of female attention and companionship. One day the brothers come to the horrible realization that one of them must marry—"horrible" because they have no idea how to meet women, let alone marry them. Harry, the eldest, is selected. After he brings home Milly, the other brothers are ready to give wedded life a try. They run into a little problem: it seems none of the local women want to marry them. Milly knows better, though. She knows that the town girls have long had their eyes on the brothers, besides being desperate to marry in a town short of men. She suspects that, if she could get the girls out to the farm to see the brothers in their natural environment, weddings would surely follow.[195]

"The Sobbin' Women" was so popular it was made into a stage musical and a movie called *Seven Brides for Seven Brothers*.[196] In 1954, the movie was nominated for an Academy Award for Best Picture.

***

By now, in New York City, the snows were beginning to melt and the spring of 1926 had arrived. With spring came the publication of the list of Guggenheim grant recipients—and Stephen's name was on it!

"Don't worry," he wrote Rosemary, who was still in Chicago. "Everything is all right."[197]

With the grant money, and the money he'd earned from the articles and short stories he'd written in the past year, Stephen could now spend a year writing that long poem—perhaps about the Civil War. And he could write it in his favorite city—Paris.

At the end of the summer, Stephen, Rosemary, and little Stephanie sailed for France. There they would soon greet a new family member, and there Stephen would write an epic poem about an epic event.[198]

The girls were always beautiful. The men
Wore varnished boots, raced horses and played cards
And drank mint-juleps till the time came round
For fighting duels with their second cousins.[199]

From *John Brown's Body*

PART SEVEN: JOHN BROWN'S BODY, PART I

Stephen's son, Thomas Carr Benét, was born on September 28, 1926. Luckily, baby Thomas waited for his parents to arrive in France, and so made his first appearance in Paris rather than aboard the ocean liner.

Everyone then settled into a happy life in a borrowed Paris apartment. Three-year-old Stephanie, who soon spoke both French and English with ease, enjoyed playing in the sand in a nearby park and chatting with the family's French cook.[200] Rosemary, in addition to tending the new baby, was writing a monthly "Letter From Paris" for *Town and Country* magazine.[201]

Stephen decided that the long poem he was to write would tell the story of America's Civil War. That war had fascinated him since he first heard his father's stories about it, back when he lived in the Benicia Arsenal.

Stephen's challenge: to make the people of the past "come alive," which they would do if he could just "dig them out of the dust."[202]

His first task, since he was dealing with a historical subject, would be, of course, research. He'd brought some books about the Civil War with him, but he was also a frequent visitor at the American Library in central Paris.

In later years, people often asked him why he went to France to write a long poem about America's Civil War. He had a two-part answer: one, it was much cheaper at the time to live in

Paris than in New York, and, two, living abroad helped him realize how strongly he felt about the United States. As he said in a letter to a friend—living abroad "intensified my Americanism."[203]

As evidence of this increased "Americanism," Stephen took a brief break from his long poem to write a short one called "American Names." "I have fallen in love with American names" the poem begins. "The sharp names that never get fat."[204]

Some of the colorful names in the poem are "Carquinez Straits"—the name of the waters that curved around his Benicia home—and "Wounded Knee," the name of a creek in South Dakota, which was the site of a massacre of peaceful Indians in 1890. The poem's final stanza reads:

> You may bury my body in Sussex grass,
> You may bury my tongue at Champmedy.
> I shall not be there. I shall rise and pass.
> Bury my heart at Wounded Knee.[205]

Later, a book by Dee Brown recounting the history of Native Americans in the American West borrowed the last line of the poem for its title. In the 1970s, Wounded Knee was the site of an Indian protest over treaty rights.[206]

Returning to his Civil War research, Stephen quite enjoyed himself. "It is worthy . . . to assemble facts, to put truth in the face of legend, to investigate impartially, to throw new light on an old problem," he later wrote in a magazine article about the writing of the poem.[207]

Finding the books he needed was a bit of a challenge. At the time Stephen was writing, the mid-1920s, few books had been written about the Civil War. And when a book of battles or the biography of a general or statesman did exist, often it had not been carefully researched.[208]

Stephen worked many hours each day. As he later explained to an interviewer: "When you set out on a long poem . . . it's not possible to write only when you are feeling fine. You have to write so much every day or you'd never get the thing done."[209] As he worked, he hoped his new poem, which he was soon calling *John Brown's Body,* had in it "some of the landscapes, sights, the sounds of the people, which are American." Yet, "every time I sit down to [write the poem] I wonder if anyone else will ever be able to read it without falling asleep." Still, "I shall finish it or explode in loud fragments of *Battles and Leaders of the Civil War.*"[210]

Finally, as the Christmas holiday approached in 1927, the poem was finished. He felt as if he'd "given birth to a grand piano."[211]

He sent the original manuscript to agent Brandt to send to Doubleday, a publisher. The carbon copy went to his parents. Stephen was particularly concerned about his father's reaction.[212] He'd thought of his father so often while writing the piece, it was almost as if his father had been beside him. Stephen remembered how steadfast the colonel was in his belief in the military creed of duty, honor, and country, and Stephen hoped he'd expressed those values to his father's standards. The colonel's descriptions of Grant, of Sherman, of Lee, had sung in Stephen's ears as he'd described these generals in his poem.[213]

Before Stephen learned his father's thoughts, he learned of the colonel's death—suddenly, of a heart attack, on March 30, 1928. About his father he said, "Nothing in life . . . can ever make up for that particular relationship . . . . He understood me completely. And he was the best man I ever knew or am likely to know."[214]

Years later, when *The Reader's Digest* asked Stephen to select some generally known figure for an article entitled "The Most Unforgettable Character I've Met," he could not accept, saying: "I'm afraid the person who influenced me most is still my father,"[215] and his father, of course, was not "generally known." *The Digest* modified their requirements and allowed him to write about his father.

Though his father was gone, Stephen did have some comfort. Before his death, the colonel had received the carbon copy of *John Brown's Body,* had read it, and had approved of it.[216]

These were your lovers in your buckskin-youth.
And each one married with a dream so proud
He never knew it could not be the truth
And that he coupled with a girl of cloud.

From *John Brown's Body* [217]

PART EIGHT: JOHN BROWN'S BODY, PART II

John Brown's Body is the story of a nation struggling to create itself. It is also the first major fictional treatment of the Civil War. It tells that story as an epic poem through the eyes of many characters—with each story in a different poetic form.

The poem begins with an "Invocation" where the poet calls upon the "American Muse" to help him write the poem. From "a hundred visions" of the essence of America, the poet explains, he hopes to make just one. To the Muse, the poet brings "a cup of silver air"—his dreams and words.[218]

The "Invocation" is followed by an opening story called a "Prelude," a gritty description of life on a slave ship. The ship's captain and his first mate attempt to justify their work, while below them human bodies are packed like cargo, wailing and sobbing. Among the crowd a woman sleeps with her dead baby, a man's eyes smolder with hate.[219]

The main part of the poem follows, a series of eight "Books" (instead of chapters). The story involves many characters, including Jack Ellyat, a young man from New England, and Clay Wingate, a young man from Georgia. The reader meets these two, their families, friends, and loves, and travels with them into battle.

Others play roles within this picture. The reader watches the President of the South tremble and eavesdrops on Lincoln's dreams, shares the adventures of the generals and their men, and meets people not in the army—the spy, the poets and writers, the house servants, the snooty southern belle, and housewife Judith Henry.

Mrs. Henry's farm becomes a battlefield in the Battle of Bull Run. The reader watches as the walls of her house and her ordinary household objects become riddled with bullets: "the brown clock in the kitchen gouged by a bullet, [while] a jar leaks red preserves on the cupboard shelf . . . ."[220]

"The guns do not look for you, Judith Henry," we are told, but "they find you . . . and leave you helplessly dying."[221] In the future, the poet tells us, visitors will drive out on

> . . . Sundays to look at the
> monument near the rebuilt house, buy picture postcards and
> wonder dimly what you were like when you lived and what
> you thought when you knew you were going to die.[222]

Perhaps the most interesting feature of the poem is that it gathers the many voices of those whose lives were touched by the war. Some examples:

From a girl on the home front, remembering a boy she once knew: "He danced with me. He could dance rather well. He is dead."[223]

From Lincoln, when the war grows tough:

> We can fail and fail,
> But, deep against the failure, something wars,
> Something goes forward, something lights a match,
> Something gets up from Sangamon County ground
> Armed with a bitten and a blunted axe
> And after twenty thousand wasted strokes
> Brings the tall hemlock crashing to the ground. [224]

And from Jack Ellyat, speaking of Melora, the girl he loves but can't find and can't forget:

> I will forget. I'll wear my riddled coat
> Fourth of Julys and have boys gape at me.
> I'll drink and eat and sleep, marry a girl;
> Be a good lawyer, wear the hunger out.
> I hardly knew her. It was years ago.
> Why should the hunger stay?[225]

We meet John Brown, a strange man who believed so passionately in ending slavery that he felt killing was justified. In Brown's day, respected people, like former slave and public speaker Frederick Douglass and writer Henry David Thoreau, did not speak against him. Some people say John Brown helped to start a bad, bloody war. Yet others say the war was necessary to end slavery. Was John Brown a hero or a monster? Perhaps both, perhaps neither, the poet suggests. And what about the world John Brown left us? The poem's last words refuse to judge it.

> Say neither . . .
> "It is a deadly magic, and accursed,"
> Nor "It is blest," but only "It is here."[226]

***

The first hint of *John Brown*'s success came with its selection by the Book-of-the-Month Club before it was published, and the large size of their first edition—65,000 copies.[227]

In August 1928, so that he would be in New York on publication day, Stephen booked a second-class passage for America. Rosemary and the children stayed behind in Paris.

As his ship neared New York harbor, a Doubleday employee rode out on a small boat with a reporter to meet the ocean liner. As Stephen told Rosemary: "The reporter interviewed me, then they took me up to the sundeck of the first class where I was photographed in every possible expression of stupid surprise."[228]

When the ship docked, more reporters met him, and even more showed up at the apartment where he was staying. The next day, when he casually mentioned to those surrounding him that he'd like to read a detective story, he was sent a dozen new ones. As his publisher explained, "If you want a white elephant . . . we'll get it for you."[229]

After a month in America, Stephen rejoined his family in France. There, for the next eight months, he enjoyed *John Brown*'s success. In its first years, 1928-1929, the book would earn more than ten times the value of the Guggenheim grant—about $25,000[230]—then provide, for the rest of his life, yearly royalties of $500 to $1000.[231] Over the years, the book continued to top best-seller lists and was used in hundreds of schools, from elementary to college. Often students wrote to Stephen for help on the term paper topic: "*John Brown's Body* as a National Epic." He received letters from fans across the country, including relatives of the real people he'd mentioned in the poem.[232]

In Atlanta, Georgia, a writer named Margaret Mitchell was working on a long novel about the Civil War. One day, her friend Frank Daniel came to visit. He was writing a newspaper review of *John Brown's Body*. Daniel praised the book and read passages from it aloud. Mitchell was so moved by what she heard that she pleaded with him to stop—fearing she'd lose the nerve to continue with her own book. Daniel kept reading, "in spite of the fact," Mitchell later recalled, "that I had flung myself on the sofa and stuck my fingers in my ears and screamed protests. I had to read it all then. The result was that I wondered how anybody could have the courage to write about the war after Mr. Benét had done it so beautifully." She got even more specific: when compared with *John Brown's Body*, Mitchell felt her own book resembled a children's book called *The Little Colonel,* later made into a movie starring Shirley Temple.[233]

Of course, Ms. Mitchell did have the courage to continue with her book. Published in 1936, *Gone With the Wind* was a national bestseller and later was made into one of the most popular movies of all time.

As World War II approached—the popularity of *John Brown's Body* continued. Famous actors read the poem on the radio, or performed it live to sell-out crowds in theatres and auditoriums. These productions included specially composed music and choruses of supporting voices.[234]

In the library near his home in a suburb of Detroit, a young African-American man named Robert Hayden read Benét's poem. While reading he took special note of Benét's statement that someday "a poet will rise to sing" the African-American experience. Hayden read those words as a call to himself. Throughout his life, Hayden wrote poetry that sought to present a true rendering of African-Americans in American history.[235] Hayden's poem "Middle Passage" describes the horrors of a slave ship on the slave trade's "middle passage" between Africa and the West Indies. Like Benét's "Prelude" to *John Brown's Body*, the tale is told largely through the eyes of the enslavers, to searing affect. Hayden would go on, in 1976, to be the first African-American to be appointed "Consultant in Poetry to the Library of Congress," a position later called the Poet Laureate.[236]

Robert Hayden, in turn, touched those who would follow him. Present day writer and poet Ta-Nehisi Coates, for example, lists Hayden as one of his influences. Coates writes that, in "Middle Passage," Hayden "could bring forth both joy and agony without literally writing the words."[237]

Two other fans of *John Brown's Body* were the Kennedy brothers John and Edward. When Senator Edward Kennedy was asked to read his favorite poems at an event at Lincoln Center in New York in 2004, he read passages from *John's Brown's Body* and explained that the poem had been a favorite of his since he discovered it in high school.[238]

President John F. Kennedy was such a fan of the poem that his wife Jackie memorized passages so they could quote the poem to each other.[239] For Christmas the year after President Kennedy died, Jackie gave their son John, Jr., a copy of the poem in which she wrote that it had been his father's favorite book.[240]

The poem's twenty-first century readers include San Quentin prisoners. A segment of Public Broadcasting System's MacNeil-Lehrer Report featured excerpts from a San Quentin performance of the poem. The documentary *John Brown's Body–at San Quentin Prison* recorded elements of the performance and includes descriptions by the prison actors of how the poem affected them. The performance and documentary director, Joe DeFrancesco, together with some of the former inmates who participated, conduct screenings of the film at community gatherings.[241]

Stephen, just past his thirtieth birthday, had become a national figure, and his poem was being called "an American Classic."[242]

While he was pleased to have so many readers, Stephen grew concerned that the poem might be used "to harry schoolboys into learning." When a later edition of the poem was published he made a point to say: "I have no quarrel with the wise, / No quarrel with [teachers]." "And yet I wrote for none of these." Instead,

> . . . if, perhaps, some idle boy
> Should sometimes read a page or so
> In the deep summer, to his girl,
> And drop the book half-finished there,
> Since kissing was a better joy,
> Why, I shall have been paid enough.
> I'll have been paid enough indeed.[243]

In the early fall of 1929, while Stephen, Rosemary and the children were preparing to move back to America, they had some friends over for dinner one Saturday night. A telegram interrupted the meal. William had sent the message: *John Brown's Body* had won the highest award it could win, the Pulitzer Prize for Poetry.[244]

"Oh, so many people are dead!" she said. "And so many don't care about living, except to be safe. I don't always want to be safe. It isn't enough."[245]

From *James Shore's Daughter*

PART NINE: GATHERING GLOOM

While Stephen and Rosemary were in France, William became a widower for the second time when his wife Elinor Wylie died. During her brief membership in the Benét family, Elinor wrote a poem entitled "Love to Stephen." In it, she captures Stephen's exuberance and youthfulness, comparing him to a host of people, animals and things, including David Copperfield, an aide to Robin Hood, a pirate, a jaguar, a Spanish sailing ship, and Davy Crockett.[246]

While Stephen and Rosemary were away, William's children had moved from the care of their grandmother and Aunt Laura to the home of their Aunt Kathleen Norris, sister of their mother Teresa. By now a successful romance novelist, Kathleen could easily care for the Benét children, whom she loved as if they were her own, along with her own two sons (one adopted, one biological).[247]

William's children were now attending boarding schools and spending summers on the Norris' large Northern California ranch. This meant, sadly, that Mrs. Benét and Laura were no longer in the children's lives. Though Laura longed to marry and have children of her own, she never did. As she explained later in her life: "Twice in my life I was very much in love. But they each married someone else."[248]

With the success of *John Brown's Body*, Stephen could take a couple of years and simply write poetry. Finally, he no longer needed to worry about earning enough money to support a wife and family. Or so he thought.

To make the money go farther, he'd invested it in "good, sound, New Era stocks" in a strong, rising stock market. Unfortunately, those "New Era" stocks crashed with the stock market in the fall of 1929, just as the family was settling into an apartment in New York.

The crash of 1929 ushered in America's Great Depression, which lasted throughout the 1930s. During these years, many people lost jobs, including many men with families to support. People sold apples on the street and stood in long lines waiting for free bread, just to have something to eat.

Despite the success of *John Brown's Body*, the stock market loss made Stephen's financial situation almost as dire as before its publication.[249]

No matter how "good" and "sound" his stocks were supposed to have been, investing in the stock market was a risk, and he had lost. Sometimes, Stephen believed, a person needed to take risks. As he once said: "Life's too brief and insecure . . . not to play everything you have on the appearance of Little Joe, even when you have no logical reason to suppose he will emerge."[250]

So he lost most of his money in the stock market; so he couldn't spend his time on poetry. Well, he had an alternative: an offer to write for the movies, a twelve-week contract, beginning in December 1929, that would pay, per week, $1,000—almost $14,000 per week in today's money. Even at the time, the $1000 per week was a substantial sum, twice as much as the weekly salary of many other movie writers.

The offer came from a famous director known for creating spectacular movies—the George Lukas/Steven Spielberg of the silent movie era—named D.W. Griffith. Griffith was a handsome, soft-spoken, older gentleman with a deep interest in the Civil War. He wanted to do a movie version of *John Brown's Body*, but his studio bosses said he could not film a poem. It did not help that, when one boss was told that *John Brown's Body* had won the Pulitzer, he responded by saying: "So, who's Pulitzer? . . . And who the hell is John Brown?" Instead, the Bosses suggested a movie about Lincoln starring Walter Huston, a respected actor.[251] Griffith agreed. The movie would be one of only two "talking pictures" directed by Griffith.[252] Stephen was asked to write the script.

Needing the money, Stephen headed to Hollywood. Unfortunately, he went without his family. He and Rosemary felt the children needed to stay where they were after their recent move from France. Stephanie would soon be entering an all-English-speaking school in New York City, while three-year-old Tommy spoke more French than English.[253]

It had been hard to leave the family with Christmas approaching. And though cold weather wasn't a problem in Southern California, when he reached Hollywood, Stephen felt he'd entered a "madhouse."[254]

In the early 1930s, to most of America, Hollywood was a magical, bigger-than-life place—the place people saw in all those amazing movies that they watched in beautiful movie palaces. The Hollywood Stephen saw, however, was quite different. As he described it in a letter to Rosemary: "[Hollywood] is one loud, struggling Mainstreet, low-roofed, mainly unskyscrapered town that struggles along for twenty-five miles or so, full of stop & go lights, automobiles, palm trees, Spanishy—& God knows what all houses—orange-drink stands with real orange juice—studios—movie theaters—everything but bookstores."

Posters for two of D.W. Griffith's silent movies.

Stephen's first stop was a room in the large, sprawling Ambassador Hotel—just across the street from the famous Brown Derby Restaurant. On his first weekend he traveled 450 miles north to visit William's son James and daughters Rosemary and Kit at Kathleen Norris' home. He felt shy with the children, as it had been a while since he'd seen them, but he reported to his wife that they were fine—happy and "perfectly charming."[255]

Reporting to the studio each morning for work, Stephen was not completely clear as to what he was supposed to be writing.[256] Soon, though, Griffith took Stephen under his wing, teaching him about Hollywood and introducing him to new people and experiences.

One of the first things Stephen learned was that Hollywood had two sides. The "party" side involved outings with Griffith. Though, physically, Griffith resembled an early 20th-century college president, or even a state governor, with Griffith Stephen found himself touring the beach scene, visiting the mansions of Griffith's millionaire friends, and stopping at nightclubs, where Griffith liked to dance.[257] Hollywood's other side involved ugly battles between the "money men"—the movie executives—and the "creative people"—the writers, directors and actors. In Stephen's view, these battles were horrible and unnecessary. The "money men" knew nothing about making movies; why couldn't they just step out of the way and let the creative people create?

After only a month of Hollywood's madness, Stephen felt that, if he didn't leave soon, he'd go crazy.[258]

Finally, Stephen's twelve weeks were over. Griffith asked him to stay for a second project, a movie about the famous shootout at the Alamo in Texas. For this movie, Stephen would have had an even higher salary, plus a percentage of the profits.[259] But he was through with Hollywood.

The end of Stephen's Hollywood stay was rather dramatic. As told by his son Tom, after Stephen had finished the *Lincoln* script, Griffith took it to the "money men." The bosses then called for a script conference, insisting that Benét be present. Stephen "sat through the long autopsy of his script without saying a word. Then he rose, looked at [Griffith], sadly shook his head, picked up his hat and left. He took the next train back to New York."[260]

The finished movie is a bit ponderous, though it does reflect Stephen's sensitivity to the human side of the Civil War era. The film shows both Lincoln and Confederate General Lee suffering, for example. Another nice touch is the prominence of Ann Rutledge; she's depicted as a sweet girl (much nicer than Lincoln's eventual wife, Mary Todd) and is presented as Lincoln's first love, and perhaps his true love.[261]

***

Returning to the gray world of New York in mid-February 1930, a place where the sidewalk trees were still bare of leaves and icy patches of snow accumulated in the gutters, within days Stephen became seriously ill with a crippling arthritis of the spine—perhaps caused in part by a weakness created by the scarlet fever he'd had as a child. The arthritis would afflict him for the rest of his life.

For the next year and a half, from early 1930 until mid-1931, doctors hovered over him, each with a different diagnosis and a variety of remedies. The only remedy that seemed to work was "sea air and quiet life" at the family's rented summer home in Peace Dale, Rhode Island.[262]

While Stephen was ill, he was not able to do much writing or make any personal appearances. One thing he could do, though, was think. A new idea for a second epic poem began tumbling around in his head. This one would be about the progress of Americans from the East Coast to the West. His summers in Peace Dale helped

Stephen and friend, possibly in Peace Dale, Rhode Island

nurture this idea. There, all around him, he saw life that was "nearer the best of early America than anywhere else," at least in his opinion.[263]

Stephen's illness was costly. In early 1931, health insurance that allowed people to pay in advance for medical care was only just beginning to be developed.[264] Stephen and his family had no help with medical expenses. Each visit to the doctor, each stay in the hospital, generated a bill that Stephen had to pay.

By mid-1931, because of his inability to work due to his illness, and because of the expense of doctors' bills, Stephen was, once again, almost broke—despite the money he'd earned in Hollywood. Needing money forced him to return to the magazine short stories he so hated. With each story he sent to his agent so that Brandt might sell it to a magazine, he felt: "Here's some light summer reading for the chewing gum trade . . . Try and get it swallowed by some large editor."[265]

Even with the sale of several short stories, by the fall of 1931, money remained tight. He still had expensive doctor bills; Stephanie and Tommy were now in private schools; and, each year, he paid a premium on his life insurance of $260 (about $4,000 in today's money). At least Brandt had not been forced to cut the sale price for his stories because of the Great Depression that now cloaked the country. There was little chance, however, that the price would rise as long as the Depression continued.[266]

A happy event for the family was the birth of a daughter, Rachel. A third child, unfortunately, required a bigger, more expensive, house.[267]

The family found a place to rent at 220 East 69th Street. Stephen described the house to a friend. It looked "like something you build out of those pink stone building blocks when you are a child." A plus was its backyard, where he could plant grass seed and tulips.[268]

Though Stephen was feeling much better, early 1932 brought more money concerns. During his long walks around the City, he saw shuttered stores on Madison Avenue and many "Out of Business" signs. William asked for a loan but Stephen had no money to lend. The Chicago bank holding his mother-in-law's comfortable savings went out of business, leaving her in need of financial help from Rosemary.

"We continue to exist," he wrote a friend. "One jump ahead of the sheriff."[269]

As she always did, Rosemary contributed what she could to the family income. She translated many books from French, including children's books, detective novels, and the works of Colette, a famous French author. In addition, she published articles and poetry in several magazines, including *The New Yorker*.[270]

There was not enough money, but Stephen simply couldn't keep writing one shallow story after another. Instead, he turned to a topic he loved—the American past—and a technique he'd used in "The Sobbin' Women"—that of having the oldest person living in a small town tell the story. These tales became known as his "Oldest Inhabitant" stories.

These stories touched on a variety of episodes in America's past. One story might be set in the pre-war South, another during the post-war Reconstruction. Another might involve a ride down the Mississippi on a flatboat, or crossing the mountains in a covered wagon. Still others dealt with clipper ships, hunting, trotting races, steamboats, or Yankee peddlers. As historically charming as these stories may have been, they were very hard, if not impossible, for Brandt to sell.[271]

If one did sell, it often won an award. Stephen had two stories named among the year's best by the people behind the O.Henry Memorial Award, the most well-known short-story prize. In 1932, his story "An End to Dreams" won the O.Henry First Place Prize.[272]

Yet, as he told his agent: "I usually have to pay the rent about the time somebody gives me a medal or a testimonial."[273] What he really could have used was a little extra cash.

Because of *John Brown's Body,* Stephen could earn money lecturing. For each lecture he'd be paid between $100 and $350.[274] Stephen's lectures were popular. He spoke to many audiences—from the young men at West Point for two days each year (plus delivering a lesson on the Civil War), to ladies' clubs in the Midwest. In between, he spoke at Harvard, Yale, New York University, and other important colleges.[275] Lectures meant being away from his family, and they always left him feeling weary or ill,[276] so much so that he really did not believe God meant for him to lecture, but "to sit on my rear and write."[277]

He did turn down the requests to speak at the schools of his friends' children. As he explained: "thirteen-year-olds floor me. I am afraid of them. As soon as I get up in front of them I begin to think how funny I look and wonder if all my buttons are properly fastened."[278]

Even with the lecture engagements, money was short. He wrote more "Oldest Inhabitant" stories but they didn't sell. "This is all perfectly mad and I have faith in the United States and Art," he wrote to his brother near the end of 1932. "But if present conditions keep on, I'm afraid I'm going to be in a hole. I should say a rather long one, too."[279]

New York Public Library
Stephen was such a frequent visitor to the New York Public Library that he wrote a poem called "Hymn of a Reader to the New York City Librarians" (reprinted in *The Village* newspaper, New York, April 10, 1952 and included in Laura's Scrapbook).

You have no fear because you have no breath.
Your silver essence knows nor cold nor heat.
Your world's beyond. My only world is here.

From "The Body complaining to the Soul"[280]

PART TEN: BODY AND SOUL

No matter how dire his own poverty, Stephen sought to help others, even those he did not know. When he learned of a young woman attempting to raise a special-needs child after her communist-poet husband had deserted her, Stephen wrote his publisher seeking a job for her in one of the company's bookstores. Apparently, the book department of a large department store had already turned her down because—since she could literally not afford enough food—"she was undernourished."[281]

By November of 1933, things were looking up. "The dead weight, the black chill of last winter, that lay on the spirit like frozen blood, is gone," Stephen wrote a friend.[282]

He was feeling better. He'd sold some short stories, including one of his "Oldest Inhabitant" tales. Over the summer, he and Rosemary had created *A Book of Americans*, a series of poems about famous Americans for children, with which he was quite pleased. Primarily, he'd written about the men, while Rosemary had written about the women. [283]

Lincoln rates a poem, of course, but so does his mother Nancy Hanks. The book includes other presidents, like Thomas Jefferson; naturalists, like John James Audubon; and pirates, like Captain Kidd:

> This person in the gaudy clothes
>   Is worthy Captain Kidd.
> They say he never buried gold.
>   *I think, perhaps, he did.*

> They say it's all a story that
> >   His favorite little song
> > Was "Make these lubbers walk the plank!"
> >   *I think, perhaps, they're wrong.*[284]

As five-year-old son Tommy sat at the end of the dining room table listening to his parents read poems for the book, his favorite was about President Woodrow Wilson:

> When Wilson was a little boy
> >   His friends all called him Tommy.
> > And so did all his relatives,
> >   His father and his mommy.[285]

A Book of Americans was a big seller and became especially popular in schools. Verses were set to music, and plays and skits based on the various poems were performed in classrooms and on school stages across the country.[286]

Another good thing happened in 1933: Stephen became the editor of Yale's yearly poetry competition, "The Yale Series of Younger Poets." Currently this prize is the oldest yearly literary award in the United States "open to any American under forty who has not previously published a volume of poetry." When Stephen was selecting the winners, the cut-off age was thirty.[287] Stephen was honored to take on this editorship, and he continued to feel grateful to the Series for publishing one of his first poetry books, *Young Adventure*.[288]

As editor of the Series, every year Stephen would read submissions, correspond with many of the poets, and select a yearly winner. The prize was publication of 500 copies of the poet's book, on which the winner would earn a royalty—a small sum for each book sold. If all copies sold, the winner would earn $100 (about $1,800 in today's money). By the second year of his editorship, knowing the economic demands on young writers, Stephen felt it was unfair that the winner had the chance of making only $100. Though his own money situation was still tight, he insisted that—rather than earning $250 for selecting the winner—he be paid only $150. With this sacrifice, the winner's prize became worth a maximum of $200.[289]

The first poet to whom Benét awarded the prize, in 1933, was Shirley Barker, who went on to publish several volumes of poetry, as well as a string of successful novels.[290] The next year's winner was a young man named James Agee, who would one day co-write the screenplay for *The African Queen*, starring Humphrey Bogart and Katherine Hepburn, and win the Pulitzer for the autobiographical novel *A Death in the Family*.[291] Agee was followed by Muriel Rukeyser, who would publish many volumes of poetry, as well as several biographies and children's books. She would also be an important activist in the areas of women's rights, labor issues and Judaism.[292]

Still another winner, in 1938, was Joy Davidman. In addition to being a poet and writer, Davidman was the beloved wife of C. S. Lewis and an influence on his writings. *The Chronicles of Narnia* books are among C.S. Lewis' most popular works.[293]

The last poet to win the prize, while Stephen was editor, was African-American poet and writer Margaret Walker. Before winning, Margaret had submitted her work three times—in 1939, 1940, and 1941—receiving encouraging letters from Stephen but not nabbing the prize.[294] Growing discouraged, she did not submit her work in 1942. When Stephen got that year's entries, however, there was nothing that struck him as outstanding. Where was that volume he had read last year by Walker? Stephen had the Walker volume resubmitted and awarded it the prize for 1942.[295] With this award, Walker became the first African-American woman to receive a national writing prize.[296]

Walker's book, entitled *For My People*, went through six editions with Yale and was one of Walker's best-known works. She is also known for writing a novel about the African-American experience of the Civil War called *Jubilee*.[297] By 1985, *Jubilee* had sold more than one million copies and was called "the Bestseller with all the sweep and grandeur of *Gone With the Wind*!" and "A Jolting Epic of Slavery."[298]

In late 1942, Stephen invited Walker to his home in New York. Famous for lateness, when Walker arrived she'd missed the party Stephen had arranged in her honor. Instead she got a tour of Stephen's writing space and the opportunity to discuss her work. According to Stephen's son Tom, after what Walker considered a "magical afternoon" was over, she "left feeling she had not just made an important connection but had found a friend as well." Sadly the two never met again, as Stephen died five months later.[299]

The tip of New York's Manhattan Island, during the time Stephen was living and working in the City.

Still another writer Stephen helped was a young man from Iowa named Paul Engle. Engle had won the Yale Series of Younger Poets prize in 1932, the year before Stephen took over the Series. The two had met when Stephen appeared at the University of Iowa on a speaking engagement. In addition to praising Engle's Yale Series winner *Worn Earth*, Stephen was instrumental in finding a publisher for the younger man's second—and breakout—work, *American Song*.[300] Engle acknowledged Benét's help by dedicating *American Song* to Stephen and Rosemary.[301]

Stephen and Engle would continue a friendship and correspondence that would last for the rest of Stephen's life. Engle would go on to transform the Iowa Writers' Workshop from a small class of eight students into an important and prestigious program. Together with his future wife, he would found Iowa University's International Writing Program.[302]

With the Iowa program, Engle, in turn, influenced a generation of writers, including short-story writer Flannery O'Conner and poet Robert Bly.[303]

At this time, Stephen's own work continued to receive awards that came with no monetary prize. After receiving the Roosevelt Medal for Distinguished Poetry, he wrote to a friend: "I don't know quite what you do with a medal . . . except carry it around in your upper breast pocket and hire somebody to shoot you in it, so you can say afterwards that it saved your life—but it is very nice of them and I am pleased to get it."[304]

During the fall of 1933, his primary writing project was the novel *James Shore's Daughter*. "Must get back to work at once for finances never worse & plans all uncertain," he noted in his diary.[305] Perhaps it's not surprising that *James Shore's Daughter* tells the story of a woman who chooses money over love.

At this point in his life, the conflict that would haunt Stephen until his death was particularly intense: he must write what would earn the quick money he needed to feed his body, but what of the poetry and stories he must write to feed his soul? Within a few years, this recurring conflict would contribute to the creation of Jabez Stone and his deal with the Devil.

Though a poet by nature, not really a novelist—not even really a short-story writer, and definitely not a hack writer—Stephen was not writing poetry. And though his greatest financial success had come from the poem *John Brown's Body*, he felt he must do the short stories, the novels, and even the hack work, because they provided money more quickly. That second epic poem about Americans moving West—now called *Western Star*—on which he wished to spend his time, was getting little attention.

He longed for the "peace & stability to do [his] own work," according to his diary, yet even when *James Shore's Daughter* was finished, he couldn't take the time to feed his soul.[306] He was in such need of money he was even willing to return to Hollywood, where he'd been so unhappy.[307]

One reason Stephen was so pressed for money was that he was attempting to live the life of his wealthy Yale classmates, most of whom had more money than he did. When he entertained them with dinners and engagements, he felt he had to do so in the same costly style in which they had entertained him and Rosemary.

To cut other costs would not have been easy. Many of the expensive trappings of Stephen's life provided real benefits. His "good New York address" kept him in the center of things, important for his career. Before the widespread use of air-conditioning, summers in Rhode Island allowed the family to escape the stifling heat of New York. Without modern appliances, Rosemary might have felt that help with daycare and housework were a necessity in a family with three children and two working writers. Stephen probably would not have minded dropping the Brooks Brothers suits. As it was, he often stuffed the well-cut pockets with papers, letters and packages. Such expensive suits were the uniforms of his world, however, and not wearing them would have been unthinkable.[308]

Then, too, education was extremely important to Stephen. He sent his three children to the best private schools, yet Rosemary often picked up the children herself, while many other families sent governesses. (One day, these ladies mistook Rosemary for a governess. For fun, as the chatty nannies grumbled about their employers, Rosemary joined the conversation, complaining enthusiastically about her "employer."[309])

Clockwise: Unknown American officer, Stephanie, the officer's wife, Stephen, Tom and Rachel. Probably a family visit to West Point, circa mid-1930s.

In addition to his money woes, Stephen was often finding it hard to hold back his thoughts while attending social functions. Despite the Depression creating poverty all around them, the wealthy people in his circle acted unconcerned. As he wrote in his diary: "[Went] to overstuffed stupid [so and so]'s for lunch. [The talk was all] where are you going for the summer? Oh, what a party we had. We missed you at Palm Beach, etc. Enormous estate. [They] have made the supreme sacrifice by opening the golf course for charity. [On the walls, expensive works of art] Goyas, etc. but God, what human beings."[310]

Later he added: "It is horrible . . . to see the nervous violence of the comfortable ones once they get the idea that one cent of their precious money is being touched. It makes you feel degraded . . . descendants of signers [of the Declaration of Independence] who talk about people on relief as if they were an inferior breed of dog. What a sorry class of rich we have here—their only redeeming feature is their stupidity."[311]

Someone who was enjoying quite a bit of success, despite the Depression, was Kathleen Norris. In January of 1935, she made the cover of *Time Magazine. Time* reported that Norris had earned roughly $300,000 in 1934 from her novels, short stories, lectures, sale of movie rights and other work. According to the magazine, Kathleen's earnings were "probably more than any other woman in the U.S." at that time.[312]

The year 1935 brought some financial relief for Stephen and his family. He'd earned some money on *James Shore's Daughter*, and Brandt had been able to sell several short stories, with help from a new editor at *Country Gentleman* magazine. He liked the "Oldest Inhabitant" tales and had bought several of them.[313] Now that Stephen had a little extra money, perhaps, finally, he could turn to work that fed his soul.

If this should change, remember the tree and the brook,
The long day's summer, the voices clever and kind,
The true verse that burned on the page of the book,
The true love, body and mind.

From "If This Should Change"[314]

PART ELEVEN: NIGHTMARES AND OTHER VISIONS

By the mid-1930s, war clouds had begun to darken the skies over Europe. Dictators—Hitler in Germany and Mussolini in Italy—were rapidly gaining power. Many Europeans were losing their freedoms; some were losing their lives.

Yet many Americans remained unconcerned. Who cared about persecutions and killings in Germany? There were no Nazis in power in America. Besides, all that talk about atrocities—those were just stories—where was the proof? And no European plane was powerful enough to fly across the Atlantic Ocean to reach America. For all these reasons, while freedoms were being suppressed and lives lost among their European neighbors across the ocean, Americans remained focused on making money and building more buildings, attempting to bring the country out of its economic depression. At least, this is the way Stephen saw the situation.

Economic recovery was important, but what did money matter when lives were being lost? In Stephen's view, Europe was not so far away, and its problems could swiftly become America's problems. "We are not an island in space," Stephen wrote. "While the air is the air, a bomb can kill your children and mine . . . . A war between nations on the other side of the globe may endanger all we love and cherish."[315]

But how to awaken a sleeping America? How to warn the nation that the dangers across the ocean were growing?

Stephen knew of only one way: writing stories and poems unlike any he'd written before. He had to turn a deaf ear to editors begging him for more "delightful stories about Southern mountaineers—or New York policemen."[316]

In contrast to his light-hearted stories, his writing now read like descriptions of nightmares. Many of his poems had the word "nightmare" in their titles: "Nightmare With Angels" and "Nightmare for Future Reference." These, and others with similar themes, he collected for a book called *Burning City*.[317]

In these poems he describes an American city that has been attacked—often, the city where he lived—New York. In reality, New York was not attacked during Stephen's lifetime. But, strangely, Stephen appears to be describing an event that did not happen until more than sixty years *after* his words were written—the terrorist attack on the World Trade Center on September 11, 2001.

In the poem "Notes to Be Left in a Cornerstone," New York City has been destroyed. An older person who remembers the living city is describing it for "you who are to come, with Time, / And gaze upon our ruins with strange eyes."[318]

In the short story "The Place of the Gods,"[319] the reader enters a time when New York has long been "The Dead Places," and the beings who once lived in it are thought to have been gods. The narrator John, the son of a priest, has a visionary flashback in which he sees "the place new york" before it was destroyed. The gods were "restless, restless . . . and always in motion! They burrowed tunnels under rivers—they flew in the air." While in their ears droned "the pulse of the giant city, beating and beating like a man's heart."

As John recounts his flashback, the fate of these beings "came upon them as they walked the streets of their city." Not like a fight in the forest, not with weapons he recognized, but with those he did not know. "It was fire falling out of the sky and a mist that poisoned. It was the time of the Great Burning and the Destruction. They ran about like ants in the streets of their city—poor gods, poor gods! Then the towers began to fall."[320]

In addition to warning his fellow Americans that their complacency while Europe was ravaged by war could lead to the destruction of their own cities, Stephen was also concerned by the growing dependence of people on machines. Might things get so bad, he wondered, that people could become the slaves of their mechanical creations? "We had expected anything but revolt," he wrote in a poetic satire called "Nightmare Number Three." "And I kind of wonder myself when they started thinking."

Yet if machines did succeed in the revolt the narrator is describing, and made people their slaves, would that be so strange? "[I]n a way, you know, we were slaves before." Cornered on a roof because the street is filled with rebellious machines, the narrator thinks about negotiating with humanity's new masters. His only real worry is something he heard about a cement mixer in Jersey: The mixer ate a person—now, was that a "mistake," "just high spirits," or—and this would be a serious problem—did the mixer "like the flavor"?[321]

As the 1930s progressed, Rosemary was also working on a story of warning. She was translating a children's book by the famous French author Andre Maurois called, in English, *Fatapoufs and Thinifers*. The book described a society of thin, aggressive people conquering a nation of plump, comfortable, yet lazy, people. Maurois wrote the book before 1930 to warn the people of France that, if they focused on ease and comfort, an aggressive enemy could conquer them. A few years later, aggressive German Nazis did conquer France.[322]

***

Soon Stephen had to stop writing his words of warning because—once again—his money was running out. Amazingly, in 1936, *The New Yorker* magazine had purchased "Notes to be Left in a Cornerstone" for the substantial sum of $418 (more than $7,000 today). This rated a special note in his diary: "Highest price ever got for a poem . . . Quite stunned."[323]

The New Yorker payment was an exception. A more typical sum he earned was $150, or about $2500 today, like that paid by the *Atlantic Monthly* for "Litany for Dictatorships."[324] During the time it took to write enough poems for his book *Burning City*, Stephen's finances had fallen so low that the $418 from *The New Yorker* was used immediately to pay overdue rent, fuel, and phone bills.[325]

The style of printer and keyboard combo, also known as a typewriter, which Stephen used in the 1930s.

*Yes, Dan'l Webster's dead—or, at least, they buried him.
But every time there's a thunderstorm around Marshfield,
they say you can hear his rolling voice in the hollows of the sky.*

From "The Devil and Daniel Webster"[326]

PART TWELVE: A DEAL WITH THE DEVIL

While their parents worried about paying the bills, the Benét children had their own concerns. For one thing, with poets for parents, there was always the risk you might be immortalized in a poem.

In "Advice to my Daughter," Rosemary described the many similarities she saw between her daughter Stephanie and her own mother. Both neatly placed their shoes by a chair each night, both favored the color yellow, and both had courage and an interest in healing. These similarities, Rosemary could accept. Yet both had a similar gaze, one that Rosemary remembered all too well from her childhood. "Choose something else, instead," she tells Stephanie.

> Inherit other virtues if you must
> But do not leave me feeling that I've spanked
> Your grandmother and sent her up to bed.[327]

Because of his mother, young Tom got pulled out of class one day to meet Andre Maurois, the author of *Fatapoufs and Thinifers,* which his mother had translated. According to Tom, Maurois "wanted to shake hands with his 'word lady's' son."[328]

Tom and his father shared an avid interest in the magazine *Astounding Stories* and other sources of science fiction. Tom and Stephen would have intense discussions on the strengths, weaknesses, and realism of many a story.[329]

Tom could never forget that his father was a writer. Since his attic bedroom was on the same floor as his father's office, many nights the boy fell asleep to the "clack, clack, clack" of his father's typewriter. Another reminder of his father's profession was the yearly reading in chapel, by the headmaster of his boarding school Exeter, of one of Stephen's most famous short stories. Despite this reading, Tom had little sense of the scope of his father's fame. So on the day his regular-guy father spoke in the school library, the boy was amazed to see the other students clamoring for his father's autograph.[330]

Stephen, in contrast, approached his visit to Tom's school with concern *because* of his fame. Might his fame, he worried, harm Tom in some way among his son's classmates? He never shared this fear with Tom—while he was alive. After his death, a magazine published one of Stephen's stories called "Famous," which described a famous father—as viewed through the eyes of his son. When reading this story, Tom felt certain the story described his father's effort to understand his son—including how Tom might have felt when his father visited his school—allowing Tom to know his father's concern one last time.[331]

Overall, Tom's main sense of his early home life was as one of "warmth, affection and stability," where his father was merely "a gentle and concerned parent," rather than the nationally known writer Stephen was at the time.[332]

***

At the end of March 1936, Stephen was still scrambling for money. "Must finish book—must also make some money," he wrote in his diary. In April, on the day he finished *Burning City*, his bank balance was down to two dollars, which even in today's money is less than $35.[333]

> Hand to mouth for last 3½ years . . . . [And] still going on.
> Should be used to it but am not—takes my courage now.
> You lose, in time, the first flair, when it's exciting to be
> broke, [and you are able to] work days at a stretch, and
> redeem finances by some coup.[334]

By July, he was so broke the family could not move to Rhode Island for the summer. "Try to work on story in evening but no go. Owe lots of money. Am so tired of things being like that."[335]

Then that deal with the Devil surfaced in his mind. No matter how deep his desperation, Stephen would never have made an actual deal with the devil, were such a thing possible, but he could—quite easily—have a short-story character make such a deal. So when Stephen had reached the place where he felt he could just throw down his pen and say—"I vow, it's enough to make a man want to sell his soul to the devil! And I would, too, for two cents!"[336] —he used his pen, instead, to write those words for the character Jabez Stone.

But what to do when the time comes for Jabez to pay up? How does one get out of a deal with the Devil? Stephen considered this. Well, how does one get out of any deal? By getting a good lawyer of course! And who would be the best lawyer to help Jabez Stone of New Hampshire? That was easy: Daniel Webster, a former United States senator from New Hampshire, famous for fiery speeches to advocate preserving the Union and abolishing slavery, before the Civil War.

Would Daniel take the case? As it happened, Mr. Webster had "about seventy-five other things to do and the Missouri Compromise to straighten out" but he agrees to help. As Daniel explained, "For if two New Hampshiremen aren't a match for the devil, we might as well give the country back to the Indians."[337]

As the story progresses, it becomes clear that the Devil is after Daniel Webster's soul as well. To save them both, Daniel must argue his case before a corrupt judge and a jury of some of the greatest villains of history. Benedict Arnold, the famous Revolutionary War traitor, is not available, as he is "engaged upon other business."[338]

When it's time for Daniel to speak, he stands ready with a fiery rage—but then he glances at the judge and jury and sees the evil in their eyes. Suddenly realizing that his own rage will only add to that evil, quickly he switches to a new plan.

Quietly, Daniel begins "with the simple things that everybody's known and felt—the freshness of a fine morning when you're young, and the taste of food when you're hungry . . ." Here, it is very likely, he begins speaking both for Jabez and to Stephen. The character Daniel says what Stephen knew but had nearly forgotten in a world that could be harsh and unforgiving. In this way Stephen reminded himself that his desperation was powerless over the might of his humanity.

Stephen has Daniel speak of America and all who helped create her, even the traitors. Daniel then turns to Jabez and shows "him as he was—an ordinary man who'd had hard luck and wanted to change it." For being a man was an endless journey, marked by failures. Men "got tricked and trapped and bamboozled." Still "it was a great journey," a journey no demon could understand, because it takes "a man to do that."[339]

Because Daniel's voice "could search the heart," and despite the terrible things they'd done, for a moment the judge and jury "were men again, and knew they were men." As men, they could understand what the Devil could not.[340]

Stephen wrote the story in ten days, called it "The Devil and Daniel Webster," and sold it to the prestigious *Saturday Evening Post* magazine as soon as it was finished. The story was published on October 24, 1936. To say it was a success would be an understatement. After its magazine appearance, the story was published as a hardcover book, going through eleven editions over the next twenty years. There were deluxe editions with fancy illustrations. It was included in many short-story collections, made into an opera and a one-act play. It even won the O.Henry Award First Place Prize, receiving the vote of every judge—a rare feat.[341]

The story not only succeeded in printed form, it also got movie attention. Two versions were made, the first in 1941, starring Oscar-winning actor Walter Huston as the Devil, which has since become a classic.

Stephen remembered that Walter Huston had appeared in *Lincoln*, the movie Stephen had written for D.W. Griffith in 1930. By now, Huston had begun to found a "Hollywood Dynasty" of sorts. In 1940, his son John directed his first movie, called *The Maltese Falcon*, and would go on to win two Oscars during his career. In a few years John would have a daughter named Angelica who would win an Oscar in a movie directed by her father.[342]

The second movie version of "The Devil and Daniel Webster," released early in the twenty-first century, starred Alec Baldwin as Jabez Stone, Anthony Hopkins as Daniel Webster, and Jennifer Love Hewitt as the Devil. Amy Poehler, Jason Patric, Kim Cattrall and Dan Aykroyd were also in the cast. [343]

For Stephen and Rosemary, happiness and relief replaced money worries for the first time in several years. More significantly for Stephen at the time, The *Saturday Evening Post* offered him a contract for four stories a year at the large sum per story of $1750 (just over $30,000 in today's dollars). A particularly nice thing about this contract was that, given the success of "Daniel Webster," these stories could be the type that Stephen wanted to write. How glorious to be able to write whatever he wanted, whether it was a story about sea serpents ("Daniel Webster and the Sea Serpent"), or leprechauns ("Daniel Webster and the Ides of March"), or more warnings about the dangers of evil governments in Europe.[344]

Roughly six months after the publication of "The Devil and Daniel Webster" Yale offered an honor Stephen was only too glad to accept—an honorary doctorate.[345] With such a degree, Stephen joined men he had long respected and admired.

The best result of "The Devil and Daniel Webster" though, was that—without having to make a deal with the Devil—Stephen's work was now in high demand, and he would earn higher fees for all his work for the rest of his life. Still, he would occasionally experience financial tension. As his earnings increased, he'd send more money to his mother—sometimes tens of thousands of dollars in today's money[346]—since she had so little to live on, and he must buy the occasional luxury for Rosemary or the children. He continued to steal time for the less financially lucrative poetry he felt compelled to write, and he could never completely stop his charitable contributions, particularly to organizations that fought tyrannical—harsh and unfair—governments. But on the strength of "Daniel Webster," his future earnings would average, each year, between the very respectable sums of $12,000 and $15,000 (around $205,000 to $257,000 today).[347]

*I have spent the last 2½ months taking notes for Western Star . . .
which really will have to get finished before I have a long white beard.*[348]

Stephen Vincent Benét in a letter to Carl Brandt,
December 26, 1939

PART THIRTEEN: WESTERN STAR

Stephen's typical day: Since he'd have been up late the night before, he'd sleep until mid-morning, then go for a walk through the streets of New York—perhaps stopping to visit a friend—and often take a ramble through Central Park. Home to four or five hours work on the short stories, the scripts, the articles—even poetry if he was free of a deadline. At mid-afternoon he'd break to spend time with Rosemary and the children as they returned from school. After dinner with the family—that was letter-writing time. Letters to friends and family, answers to fan letters, responses to advice requested by other writers. Some evenings might see dinner delayed so that he and Rosemary could throw a cocktail party to introduce a new writer to Stephen's writing and publishing friends. Other nights, dinner would be served early so that he and Rosemary could attend the theater—either a Broadway play or a movie, perhaps a premiere at Radio City Music Hall.[349]

Because Stephen was a writer, his income tended to be inconsistent. Had he wanted a more consistently profitable occupation, even before his "Devil and Daniel Webster" success, he could have chosen from a variety of impressive jobs, including Consultant of Poetry at the Library of Congress, the editor of *Fortune Magazine*, Librarian at the University of Rochester. He was flattered that he was considered worth roughly $15,000[350]—just over $248,000 today—per year on the open market. With a steady job he could have earned a regular salary. Yet a job would take away his freedom to write what he felt he must, when he felt the need. So, although taking a steady job might have helped him to avoid things like this—"Rental company writing me angry letters"—he remained a free-lance writer.[351]

The lack of a regular income, coupled with the need to balance work, family and social pressures, was taking a toll. During 1939 Stephen spent several weeks in the hospital recuperating from a nervous condition most likely due to the stress of work, money worries, and concern about the coming war in Europe. In addition, the spinal arthritis, which first surfaced after he had spent time in Hollywood writing that movie about Lincoln, was growing worse. Simply moving his neck was painful, and his hands were often twisted in pain.[352] Then, too, his health habits were poor. Typical of the time, he was a smoker.[353] During the late 1930s and early 1940s, the standard diet of a New York City dweller revolved around meat and potatoes, with no emphasis on large amounts of fresh fruit and vegetables.

Despite his need for money and his continuing bodily pain from the crippling arthritis, he was determined to write his second epic poem, *Western Star*, which would describe the western exploration of America. To help with the writing, he asked his publisher to create a map for him of the many routes west, including Daniel Boone's Wilderness Road, the Oregon and Santa Fe Trails, the tracks of the Union and Southern Pacific Railroads, and even the Lincoln Highway—which was, at the time, before coast-to-coast super highways, the most modern cross-country road.[354]

Originally he'd planned to begin with the landing of Columbus.[355] Deciding to save some time, he eliminated about a hundred years by starting with the first English colonies, Jamestown and Plymouth. The poem would end with the death of Sitting Bull in 1890.[356]

He planned to write four to ten "books," or chapters, for the poem. Each one would cover a specific aspect of Western migration. An early book would discuss Jamestown and Plymouth, while later books were meant to cover such topics as the Lewis and Clark Expedition, adventurers lured by the California Gold Rush, efforts to build the Transcontinental Railroad, and Sitting Bull leading the Lakota Nation west from South Dakota and clashing with General Custer at Little Big Horn.

One publishing executive saw *Western Star* as the natural companion to *John Brown's Body*. Perhaps remembering that *The New York Times* had described *John Brown's Body* as "an American *Iliad*," this executive added that Stephen's first epic was "the *Iliad* of our country, [and *Western Star* would be] the *Odyssey*."[357] Comparing Stephen's epic poems to classical Greek epics was appropriate. Both the *Iliad* and *John Brown's Body* recount a great war, and both the *Odyssey* and *Western Star* describe a great journey.

Like many epic poems, *Western Star* begins with an "Invocation" where Stephen explains for whom he has written this poem: all the nameless, numberless people who built the West with their energy and their lives. He then tells why he's written the poem: so that we shall remember them. This invocation includes a tribute to Stephen's Benicia boyhood. He describes the geographic scope of the great Western journey as reaching "from Jamestown to Benicia."[358]

Part of the charm of *Western Star* was its lighthearted tone, coupled with Stephen's humorous asides to the reader. Referring to the errors of the early settlers in Jamestown, he commented: "And we would all have done better—no doubt of that." He described the first settlers as if he and the reader were among them: "We would have known which Indians were friendly. (Let's hope we know as much of the Martians.)"

To help his modern readers understand the first settlers in Jamestown, he described them as "a crew / Made of ex-soldiers, fledgling aviators, / Truckdrivers, furniture-salesmen, drugstore clerks, / Machinists, workmen, a radio-announcer / And a sprinkling of nice clean boys from Yale or Harvard."[359]

While writing the Jamestown material for *Western Star*, Stephen sent a progress note to Brandt: "Conditions are rather unsettled here at Jamestown, but with God's will we yet hope to plan a nation."[360]

As with *John Brown's Body*, Stephen had some trouble researching his subject: "I wish prominent historians wouldn't contradict each other as much as they do," he told Brandt. "How's a poor poet to know which is right?"[361]

He'd been planning *Western Star* since 1930. Perhaps it is not surprising that by 1937, on his 39th birthday, he felt an extreme sense of urgency. On that day he wrote in his diary: "Must have ½ *Western Star* completed by 40."[362] Unfortunately, not only would he miss this goal, but, two years later in 1939, he was still far short of it.

In the summer of 1940, his mother died. He felt deep grief to know that her loving presence was no longer in the world, the old days of his childhood now completely gone. Again he was reminded that time was passing.[363]

And he was losing time for *Western Star*. The short stories, the lecture-readings, the occasional movie work had to take at least some of his time, because they all provided income. Then there were the favors to friends and his work with young writers, which was difficult to limit, but he had to try. Agent Brandt did what he could to help, reviewing old stories that had not yet sold and sending them off again to editors. Often, thanks to "The Devil and Daniel Webster," these stories sold, occasionally to the same editors who had rejected them five or six years earlier.[364]

Now something even more pressing than *Western Star* was entering his life. The time was coming when the nightmares he'd described in his poetry during the mid-1930s might actually come true. As war clouds darkened, he wrote to Brandt: "I think why the hell write about . . . early history . . . with the world blowing up?"[365]

With America about to enter the Second World War, Stephen put the manuscript of *Western Star* in a safe deposit vault.[366] Only the Invocation, Prelude, and Book One were in close to publishable form. The time he could spare from making a living could no longer be used for a long poem about America's history. Instead, his time must be used to serve America in her time of greatest need.

*"For, though I couldn't fight, I was a fighter...
I have been a soldier of humanity!"*[367]

From "They Burned the Books," Radio Play

PART FOURTEEN: SOLDIER WITH A TYPEWRITER

As war moved closer and closer to America, Stephen couldn't help but remember his old military dreams, how he'd longed to attend West Point like his father and grandfather, and his attempt to sneak into the Army by memorizing that eye chart back in college.

A country needs many types of soldiers. If he could not join the armed forces, he could still aid America's fight by doing what he did best—writing. His duty was so clear that he had trouble understanding how any writer could feel differently. To him "the issue . . . is between life and a certain chance to do your work and get it done—and death and no chance to get it done."[e]

While war crept over the world, he paid attention. Daily, he read the morning newspaper, then listened to hourly newscasts, ending the day by spending a large part of the evening by the radio.[368]

His war-related tasks were many and varied. They ranged from writing words for a memorial marker, to narrating a Victory Front radio program; from attending air raid meetings, to writing a pledge of allegiance for Civil Defense workers.[369] The most important war work he did, in his view, were his radio scripts.

---

e. Fenton 356-357. Many writers agreed with Stephen, using their writing skills to help with the war effort. (See e.g. "Pearl Harbor Fiftieth Anniversary Issue" of *Life Magazine* 1991.) Stephen's belief in this work was so strong, however, that both the quality and quantity of his efforts were exceptionally high.

In the late 1930s and the 1940s, radio, despite its small number of channels, was the primary electronic home source for entertainment and information, which in our day are available through hundreds of radio, television, and cable channels; DVDs; streaming services; and Internet search engines. Each radio program had a greater impact and reached a larger percentage of the population than would any single television program today. As a result, Stephen's radio scripts would be heard, not by a fragment of the country, but by most Americans. Many of Stephen's radio scripts were for government or patriotic organizations like the Council for Democracy, whose objective was to produce media material designed to educate Americans on the value of democracy.[370]

In November 1940, despite the strong possibility of war, America was bitterly divided. President Roosevelt was running for a third term—something no president had ever done. Some people believed Roosevelt wanted to become a dictator, and this made them angry.

The Council asked Stephen to write a speech to help heal the country, to be read at a rally at Carnegie Hall in New York City, the day after the election. Raymond Massey, the former major who had conducted military drills at Yale when Stephen was a student there, would read the speech. Massey was now a respected actor, nominated that year for an Oscar for his performance as Abe Lincoln in a popular movie.[371]

The speech was called "We Stand United." "We cannot be a house divided," says the speech. A house "divided in will, divided in interest, divided in soul. We cannot be a house divided and live."[372]

The speech was broadcast nationally and received national press as a major news story. "Front page of [*The New York*] *Times*," Stephen noted in his diary, "talks about my 'Lincoln-like words.' Well, well."[373]

A few months later, on May 18, 1941—called I-am-an-American-Day—Stephen's most recent poem, "Nightmare at Noon," was read over the radio. The poem described a pleasant, safe New York City:

> An airplane drones overhead but no one's afraid.
> There's no reason to be afraid in a fine, big city
> That was not built for war.

It then named the rights the American people often took for granted, like liberty, equality, and justice, and asked: "What if [those rights] pass and are gone and are no more?"[374] The poem, like his earlier "Nightmare" poems, was a warning—such rights were rapidly vanishing across the ocean, and they could be lost in America as well.

For the Fourth of July 1941, the Council asked him to write a special broadcast. He wrote a play in verse called "Listen to the People."[375] The idea here, according to Milton Krantz, Radio Director for the Council for Democracy, was for Stephen to "reflect the true feelings of Americans [in response] to the Nazi and Fascist threat to the world and would sort of project into the future what would happen to Americans if they did not recognize the dangers of Nazism to America."[376] In the play, a "Totalitarian Voice" soothingly says: "I never play upon a people's strength. I play upon their weaknesses and fear . . . [I use] all envy, all despair, all prejudice / For my own work . . . [and] what have you got to bet against my bet?"[377]   Stephen answers by writing another warning: A black storm was filling the sky, and the people of America had to see it and face it:

>But we've ridden out storms before and we'll ride out this one,
>Ride it out and get through.
>It won't be done by the greedy and the go-easies.
>The stuffed shirts, the "yes but" men and the handsome phonies,
>. . .
>It'll be done by the river of the people,
>The mountain of the people, the great plain
>Grown to the wheat of the people,
>. . .
>It'll be done by the proud walker, Democracy,
>The walker in proud shoes.[378]

By the summer of 1941, even though the problems in Europe were obvious to many, America had not yet entered the war. This meant that, officially, America was still neutral—not yet taking a stand against Hitler. Therefore, amazingly, several radio executives did not want to broadcast lines in "Listen to the People" that were offensive to Hitler. For one thing, an offended Hitler might limit America's marketing opportunities with Germany. The "offensive" words:

>You mean to tell me
>A little shrimp like that could run the world,
>A guy with a trick moustache and a bum salute . . . ?

Stephen settled the matter by making it clear that if the lines weren't read on the air, the play could not be presented. The words were read as written.[379]

Anger fueled Stephen's writing of "Listen to the People." Anger at the failure, in his mind, of many of his contemporaries to understand that government was *the people* and not "something high-sounding and far-off and scary that gets after you with a club." Government was people elected by the people and not "something some man from Mars called a 'politician' does to you."[380]

"Listen to the People" aired on the NBC radio network on July 4, 1941, just before a live address by President Roosevelt. A few days later, the play appeared in the July 7th issue of *Life* magazine. Given the timing of the broadcast and the massive circulation of *Life*, "Listen to the People" was heard or read by more Americans than the work of any other serious writer, at that time, in the history of the United States.[381]

***

Given Stephen's popularity as a patriotic writer, one might expect that the coming war was providing him with an economic boon. Yet Stephen would never even have considered profiting from his country's crisis. His messages usually expressed his own heartfelt beliefs, and so he refused to accept payment for them. If he could not avoid being paid, he sent the money to the USO (the United Servicemen's Organization) or the Army Fund. He instructed his agent to give all his English wartime royalties to the SpitFire Fund. When questioned about this decision, he said simply, "I couldn't do anything else."[382] After his death, some lines of poetry found with his papers gave a deeper view of his thinking:

> Now for my country that it still may live,
> All that I have, all that I am I'll give.
> It is not much beside the gift of the brave
> And yet accept it since tis all I have.[383]

Stephen's resolve to refuse money for his war work held firm, even though that work kept him from earning a living. About the time "Listen to the People" aired, for example, he noted in his diary: "No money, and owe more than in a long time." Yet when he received a check for $500 (about $8,000 today) from *Life,* after it published "Listen to the People," he sent the check directly to the USO.[384]

Brandt tried to help. Once again, he dug up unsold stories to sell.[385]

One of the new short stories Stephen did have a chance to write and sell, despite his war work, was "Freedom's a Hard Bought Thing." This story described for modern America the plight of a pre-Civil-War slave and his desperate desire for freedom.[386] The story triggered many letters of thanks from slave descendants, including one grandson who told Stephen of the mud-packed bells in his grandfather's collar—to silence them as he fled his pursuers.[387]

"Freedom's a Hard-bought Thing" became a radio play and earned Stephen his third O. Henry Memorial Award First Place Prize and his seventh O. Henry award overall.[388]

This story was important for another reason. With this story, Stephen put a spotlight on the treatment of blacks in a segregated America, years before a young Montgomery, Alabama, preacher named Martin Luther King, Jr., would spark the Civil Rights movement of the late 1950s and the early 1960s. In one of King's essays, called "Testament of Hope," King references the title of Benét's story, saying:

> Stephen Vincent Benét had a message for both white and
> black Americans in the title of a story, "Freedom Is a Hard
> Bought Thing." When millions of people have been
> cheated for centuries, restitution is a costly process.

King used Benét's title to explain that blacks had been forced to suffer with poor housing, inferior education, inadequate health care, and few job opportunities for years. True freedom would not come for them until these problems were solved. Correcting even one of these problems, however, would be an arduous, costly—"hard-bought"—process. [389]

Another way in which Stephen helped to amplify the voices of African-Americans, in the years before the Civil Rights Movement, was his work with young African-American writers, each struggling to find his or her writer's voice. One such writer was female poet Pauli Murray. Ms. Murray would later become a lawyer, America's first black woman Episcopal minister, a founder of the National Organization for Women (NOW), and a Civil Rights activist. In the early 1940s, she was among the first to challenge "Whites Only" laws on buses and in restaurants. In the 1960s and 1970s, she helped challenge similar laws in the U.S. Supreme Court.[390]

In the late 1930s Murray began a long correspondence with then First Lady Eleanor Roosevelt, primarily about social justice issues. In 2016, this correspondence became the subject of the book *The Firebrand and the First Lady: Portrait of a Friendship* by Patricia Bell-Scott.[391]

In 1939, Ms. Murray wrote a manuscript describing blacks trying to get front seats in a bus—sixteen years *before* Rosa Parks's famous civil disobedience in 1955. While reviewing Ms. Murray's manuscript, Stephen wrote: "Give me a line on the police. Show me the bus-driver's face. Let me see the people on the bus . . . ." As a writer, she had to get people interested in her characters, he explained. "If I read in the paper that John Smith has died of pneumonia, I think 'Too bad' and forget it. If I read . . . that a friend of mine has died of pneumonia, I feel shocked and sorry."[392] Murray's characters must feel like friends to her readers.

As 1941 progressed, because he had "absolutely no money," Stephen had to borrow a large amount from a friend—$1,000 (over $16,000 in today's dollars); but then the popular Book-of-the-Month Club decided to issue a new two-volume collection of his poetry and fiction—to be published in 1942. Eventually, over several years, he and his family would receive $9,000 (or more than $131,000 in today's dollars) for this collection.[393]

By the fall of 1941, it was clear that Stephen's health was growing worse. His arthritis was becoming particularly crippling and he began to look extremely ill. About himself, when only in his early forties, he wrote: "I am old, I am arthritic . . . I am a ruined tower."[394]

Like Stephen's health, America's peace was faltering. Already the country had begun adding soldiers to the Army and had asked farmers to grow more food. Yet—if America were to enter the great war that was growing larger and encircling the world—when, and how, would it happen?

We have made mistakes and many errors. But we have made a nation of free men, self-ruled, where each man might worship God in his own way, speak his mind in his own way, and live in neighborborliness with neighbors of every stock and creed.

From "The American Dream" by Stephen Vincent Benét[395]

PART FIFTEEN: THE AMERICAN DREAM

What is the greatest cost of war? Loss of life, of course, but wars do more than kill people. Warring nations can take away freedoms and ways of life. Most modern American wars have taken place many miles from America. There has been little risk of an invading army reaching our shores. The war on terrorism, though, has shown how an enemy can attack us on our home ground, taking lives and chipping away at freedoms.

Stephen Vincent Benét held America's freedoms close to his heart. This is why the rumblings of war pained him so deeply. Since his earliest writings, Stephen had looked to the great "Dream" America represented to the world. In the Invocation of *John Brown's Body*, he described America's early explorers as bringing a "dream so proud" to this new land.

As the war grew closer, Stephen's focus turned to just what it was that inspired Americans to fight fiercely and to die willingly for their country. If this thing was the American Dream—well, what exactly was that dream?

Some recent definers of the American Dream include the writer Ta-Nehisi Coates and the musician and songwriter Bruce Springsteen. To a young Coates, the Dream was to grow rich and live in the suburbs, perhaps in a cul-de-sac where "they staged teen movies and children built treehouses."[396] For singer/songwriter Bruce Springsteen, the Dream is not so much that everyone would become rich but "that everyone was going to have an opportunity and the chance to live a life with some decency and a chance for some self-respect."[397]

To Stephen, the American Dream had little to do with material success and buying stuff. Stephen valued economic success, but such success was something the Dream allowed, rather than the Dream itself.

Stephen understood that the American Dream must be lived by people, and that people are not always perfect. As one writer explained, Stephen "was the sort of poet who looked into the hearts of men and women and saw good and great aspiration struggling with the weeds of selfishness and fear."[398]

Perhaps because of this ability to see into hearts, Stephen knew the people would need reminding about the Dream they were fighting for, as world war intensified. With his closing words in *Listen to the People*, Stephen wrote:

> Out of the flesh, out of the minds and hearts
> Of thousand upon thousand common men,
> . . .
> We made this thing, this dream.
> . . .
> This peaceless vision, groping for the stars,
> Not as a huge devouring machine
> . . .
> But as live earth where anything could grow,
> . . .
> Grow and be looked at, grow and live or die.
> . . .
> We made it and we make it and it's ours.
> We shall maintain it. It shall be sustained.[399]

To spread this message even further, the complete closing speech in "Listen to the People" was printed as a single sheet, appropriate for posting in homes and offices.

Building on this, Stephen gathered together the beliefs that made up the American Dream and presented them in "A Creed for Americans." Some of those beliefs:

> We believe in the dignity of man and the worth and value
> of every living soul, no matter in what body housed . . . .
>
> We believe that we have a great and priceless heritage as a
> nation—not only a heritage of material resources but of
> liberties, dreams, ideals, ways of going forward.
>
> We believe it is our business, our right and our inescapable
> duty to maintain and expand that heritage.

> We believe that such a heritage cannot be maintained by the lackluster, the selfish, the bitterly partisan or the amiably doubtful. We believe it is something bigger than party, bigger than our own small ambitions. We believe it is worth the sacrifice of ease, the long toll of years, the expense of our life's blood.
>
> Most of all, we believe in democracy itself—in its past, its present and its future—in democracy as a political system to live by—in democracy as the great hope in the minds of the free.[400]

For an early wartime Thanksgiving, Stephen described the American Dream as the dream "that struggles and falters and goes forward and looks forward." And as long as Americans followed that dream, "we shall go on after this war to a new birth of freedom. We shall help and play our part in the making of a future as great as it is as yet unguessed. We shall abandon no freedom that is ours today, we shall assert other freedoms, as essential to our modern age, that have not yet come to pass [and] we shall build as we have never yet built."[401]

Believing in the American Dream as he had described it, and would describe it until the end of his life, Stephen faced the treacherous future he long knew had been coming.

Life can be lost without vision but not lost by death,
Lost by not caring, willing, going on,
Beyond the ragged edge of fortitude
To something more—something no man has seen.

From "A Child Is Born," radio play[402]

PART SIXTEEN: WAR

On Sunday December 7, 1941, Stephen spent the day working on an article for the *Herald Tribune* about Carl Sandburg, a poet who would win three Pulitzer Prizes during his lifetime. Stephen worked without the radio on, as he was past deadline, finishing up just before 6 PM. Sending the article off with a Western Union boy, Stephen poured himself a glass of vermouth and sat down in his favorite chair. Ten minutes later the phone rang.

That morning Japanese planes had bombed Pearl Harbor Naval Base in the Hawaiian Islands, the anxious caller told him.[403] The unthinkable, to many, had happened—war had touched America on her home ground. Stephen was shocked, but to him the event was not unthinkable. "And, always, the airplanes might come and the world end," he'd written in a novel eight years before.[404]

Now, as Stephen had urged in his poetry and radio scripts, the country was ready to fight to protect Democracy. As Stephen described his feelings, listening to the December 7th radio broadcasts, "you could feel the country harden and come together, like ice forming on a pond . . . There wasn't any question about it or any discussion. You just felt it in your skin like a chemical change."[405]

The next day, President Roosevelt declared the United States at war with both Japan and Germany. Unfortunately, while America had waited, Hitler and others had killed millions of people and taken freedoms from many millions more.

In early 1942, Stephen was asked to prepare a broadcast for the ninth anniversary of Hitler's burning of the books.[406]

Burning books had been one of Hitler's first acts. Like many tyrants, he recognized the importance of books to provide knowledge and stimulate ideas, so that people who read them are harder to control. The book burners:

> . . . know, if you take the children of a country
> And teach them nothing but lies about the world,
> . . .
> Give them no books that show another side,
> No word of all the words that speak for freedom,
> The man who grows from the child will believe the lies
> And never hear the truth.[407]

On Flag Day, June 14, 1942, Franklin Roosevelt read an address to the United Nations over the radio. He closed with a prayer Stephen had written:

> We are all of us children of earth—grant us that simple
> knowledge. If our brothers are oppressed, then we are
> oppressed. If they hunger, we hunger. If their freedom is
> taken away, our freedom is not secure.[408]

Since April of the same year, Stephen had been working on six programs for a series called *Dear Adolf*. The goal of this series, according to Stephen's friend Milton Krentz, the radio director for the Council for Democracy who had asked Stephen to prepare the letters, was "to help crystallize for Americans exactly what they were fighting for and to help them over a confusing period."[409]

Each *Dear Adolf* program was a letter from an American to Adolf Hitler, read by famous actors like Academy Award winners William Holden, James Cagney, and Helen Hayes. The series included letters from a farmer, a businessman, a housewife and mother, a soldier, a worker, and a foreign-born citizen.[410]

The housewife and mother had some strong words for Adolf. After all, he'd called her selfish, pampered, thoughtless, and lazy.[411] In reply, the mother tells him:

> You have stretched your hands at our children.
> And there is blood on your hands.
> . . .
> This is our war . . . not only our men's, and we mean to fight it,
> As you shall see, Adolf Hitler.[412]

These letters aired in July and August 1942 and were critically acclaimed and enthusiastically accepted by listeners. Radio executives wanted Stephen to write more letters. But since he didn't want to destroy the idea by overdoing it, he said no.[413]

While the letters aired, Stephen's "'Dear Adolf' a U.S. Soldier Writes Hitler Why His Pals are Fighting" was published in a July issue of *Life Magazine*, with the ships of America's Atlantic convoy on the cover. The story was illustrated with photographs of the faces of American fighting men.[414]

That summer, the public was also getting Stephen's words in some new books. The two-volume boxed set of *The Selected Works of Stephen Vincent Benét* was the featured Book-of-the-Month Club selection for July and August. An English professor at Columbia University reviewed the work: "Our contemporary literature and our national consciousness are both very much the better for Mr. Benét's *Selected Works*."[415]

***

While writing the "Dear Adolf" letters, Stephen relaxed with his family in the old whaling town of Stonington, Connecticut. The previous year they had finally been able to purchase a summer home of their own. Their new place was known as "the Whistler House" because the painter James Whistler, famous for his portrait of his mother, had lived there as a child.[416]

An early World War II recruitment poster.

The Whistler House, home of Stephen and his family, in Stonington, Connecticut

Helping with the purchase of the house were the higher fees he'd been receiving since "The Devil and Daniel Webster." Also, he'd recently been paid for a draft of the screenplay for a movie called "Cheers for Miss Bishop." Based on the novel by Bess Streeter Aldrich, the book and movie tell the story of a woman who devotes her life to the teaching profession, while raising the daughter produced when her fiancé runs off with her cousin, who dies in childbirth.[417]

Stephen loved Stonington, and the local residents liked and admired him. "They see me going down the street," he told a friend. "And they say: 'There goes Benny, the poet. He's thinkin'."[418]

In the fall of 1942, he wrote two more patriotic radio programs, including "A Child Is Born," a Christmas program. In "A Child Is Born," a play in verse, an innkeeper and his wife discuss the Roman tyrants ruling their country. The play does not offer an easy answer to overcoming tyrants. A thief, reformed by the birth of a child in the inn's barn, tells the innkeeper and his wife: "Tyrants will not be gone"

> 'til each one of us is willing . . .
> To hang upon a cross for every man
> Who suffers, starves, dies
> Fight his sore battles as they were our own,
> And help him from darkness and the mire.[419]

During this time, both Stephen's brother William and his sister Laura were busy with their own writing careers. William was still editing the respected literary magazine the *Saturday Review of Literature* and had just won the year's Pulitzer Prize for poetry for an autobiographical epic poem called *The Dust Which is God*.[420] Laura was writing her biographies, novels, and poetry for young people and would publish more than thirty books by the end of her life.

Laura's first biography described the boyhood of the romantic poet Percy Bysshe Shelley. Shelley was quite popular with Benét women. Laura dedicated her book to her mother, since Mrs. Benét had adored Shelley. Elinor Wyle, William's second wife, had written two novels based on the poet.[421] Perhaps this affection came, in part, because Shelley had pointed out that, while the world could probably survive quite nicely without its philosophers, "it exceeds all imagination to conceive what would have been the moral condition of the world" without its poets. This is so because, in Shelley's view, "Poetry creates for us a being within our being."[422]

Relaxing on the back porch, circa early 1940s. From left: Stephen, a family friend, Rosemary, Tom, and Stephanie.

As 1943 approached, Stephen's health was still shaky. His doctors canceled an official assignment to England he'd been given and told him, flatly, that he could not accept the major's commission the U.S. Army now offered.[423] Finally, he had his chance to join the Army, but now it was his weak body that kept him out.

He was still writing, though. On Lincoln's birthday, February 12, Raymond Massey read words Stephen had written about Lincoln over the radio.[424]

Stephen was also busy on an important project for the Office of War Information—a 40,000-word history of the United States called *America*. This work would be published in 1944 in almost every living language, with copies distributed throughout Europe and Asia. *America* gave tens of thousands of foreigners, many still impacted by war, their first description of America's history and principles.[425]

Though Stephen's war work was moving forward, his health continued to fail. On February 18, 1943, he suffered a heart attack, spending a week in the hospital.[426] In early March he was scheduled to read a two-minute statement he'd written, called "Freedom From Want," over the radio. The program would also include a dramatization of *John Brown's Body.* He did not feel well enough to go to the studio, however, so someone else read the statement while he listened at home. Afterwards, he called the studio to tell the producers the program was one of the best directed and produced that he'd ever heard.[427]

A few days later, he was feeling much better and had begun to sketch out a patriotic Easter radio show describing Christ's resurrection called "Watchers by the Stone," for which, of course, he would not be paid.[428]

Since America's entry into the war, Stephen's patriotic work had kept him from writing the short stories and novels he needed to sell to earn money for his family. Now his poor health was also limiting his ability to earn. As a result, like in the dark days of the Depression back in the 1930s, Stephen was again scrambling to earn money.

Then, on March 9, he filled out his income tax form for the previous year, 1942. That night he wrote in his diary: "discover to my horror I will have to pay about $8,000 [more than $110,000 in today's dollars], when I haven't got it. Well, well. Drink [sic] some claret [a friend] brought—very good."[429]

Ironically, although Stephen had spent much of 1942 working on projects for his country for which he took no money, he now owed the government an amount equal to almost half his income in a successful year. Much of the money he'd been paid—even if he'd donated it to a war cause—was considered income, for which he had to pay an income tax.

He was ill, he was working to his limit to earn his living and serve his country, and he owed that country over $8,000—nearly $110,000 in today's dollars! The pressures were building. Would something break?

God of the Free, . . . grant us the wisdom and the vision to comprehend the greatness of man's spirit, that suffers and endures so hugely for a goal beyond his own brief span.

From "Prayer"[430]

PART SEVENTEEN: FALLEN SOLDIER

Three days after preparing his income taxes, on Friday, March 12, 1943, Stephen told Rosemary he was ready to begin the actual writing phase of "Watchers by the Stone." After reading and rereading the four Gospels describing the Resurrection, he was convinced that the disciples had all seen the same thing at Christ's tomb.[431]

That evening he spent a pleasant time with Rosemary and his daughters—Stephanie, home from Swarthmore College for the weekend, and eleven-year-old Rachel. Son Tommy was away at his boarding school, Exeter. There were no games of charades that night—instead the family played records and talked of the latest events in the girls' lives before they all went off to bed.

To view that quiet family scene from the perspective of the 21st century, we might marvel that, because the father had chosen to spend his life as a writer and poet—and in particular a writer and poet of, and for, America—he would go to bed worried because he was deeply in debt to America's tax authority, the Internal Revenue Service. At the same time, since that man had spent his life as a writer and poet, he might have also sensed that he was one of the most famous, most beloved, and most admired men in the country.[432]

In March 1943, Stephen's poems and short stories were appearing frequently in major magazines. Radios were broadcasting his wartime scripts as well as readings of his poetry, interspersed with their Big Band broadcasts and radio serials. Speeches Stephen had written, including his words for President Roosevelt, were often broadcast and got coverage in newspapers.

In homes and on newsstands across America—in the issue dated the next day—were copies of the *Saturday Evening Post* containing the fourth installment of its series "Depicting the Four Freedoms for Which We Fight." The "Fourth Freedom" was the Freedom From Fear, with a text provided by Stephen, and the illustration of two parents tucking their children safely into bed, by Norman Rockwell.[433]

Stephen's *John Brown's Body* had remained on bestseller lists, and the year before a special annotated edition for high schools had been published.[434] The two-volume boxed set of *The Selected Works of Stephen Vincent Benét* had recently arrived in many homes from the Book-of-the-Month Club. The previous November, *House & Garden Magazine* had done a story with photos of the family at home in Stonington. In honor of the previous Thanksgiving, *The Country Gentleman* had printed Stephen's description of "The American Dream," a reminder—illustrated with images of pilgrims, pioneers and soldiers—of the greatness of the people who had created America, and the importance, in the current war, for free people "to hang together," so that they would not "all undoubtedly hang separately." Meanwhile, a new ballet by a premier New York company had called its latest production "The Nightmares of a Dictator," echoing the titles of Stephen's "Nightmare" poems, which included "Litany of a Dictator."[435] And the Hollywood movie *The Devil and Daniel Webster*, after opening with splashy news coverage, had played to large audiences just a little more than a year earlier.[436]

***

At about 3 o'clock Saturday morning Stephen woke up suddenly. He had an intense pain in his chest. He woke Rosemary. Immediately, she ached for him—but what could she do? No 911 emergency phone system yet existed. As he cried out, she took him in her arms and held him, feeling each stabbing pain as if it were in her own body. And so they lay, through several minutes of agony, until he died from the heart attack. He was forty-four years old.[437]

"If we die, what matter?" Stephen had written in a poem some years earlier. "There was a ghost in the flesh, / A ghost that went and came."[438]

Later that morning, in her grief, Rosemary went to Stephen's desk and found the New Testament with a marker at the end of the Gospel according to John. There were two sheets of yellow paper bearing all he had yet written of "The Watchers by the Stone" radio script. The first sheet contained only the title, underlined. On the other were some notes:

> 30 pieces of silver
> Earthquake
> Joseph's own tomb
> Day before Sabbath
> Put in tomb
> Resurrection occurred Monday.

Of course it's impossible to know what Stephen was thinking when he wrote that the "Resurrection occurred Monday" rather than on Sunday, according to the Bible, creating the first Easter Sunday. An event that did occur on a Monday, the one following his death, was his funeral.[439]

Stephen was buried in the Stonington Cemetery.[440] As befitted a fallen soldier, a former West Point Army chaplain officiated at his funeral.[441] On the day of the funeral, many of the nation's newspapers ran editorials, and a telegram arrived from the White House.[442] President Roosevelt wrote: "The world of letters has lost one of its most commanding figures."[443]

Stories praising Stephen appeared in newspapers across the country. A reporter at the *Kansas City Star* wrote: "The eyes of his heart and spirit could see around the world and to the stars."[444]

Joy Davidman, one of the Yale Poets with whom Stephen had worked, wrote: "I do not speak for myself alone when I say his poetry was exactly that which . . . young poets of this America would sell their souls to write."[445]

One interesting response to his death was the number of poems that appeared about him by grieving fans in the months and years after his death. One example includes the line: [He knew] "that the blind heart is worse than the blind eye."[446]

Among the many notes of sympathy Rosemary received was one from writer/lawyer/civil rights activist Pauli Murray. Speaking for all the writers Stephen had helped, she wrote, "He has scattered fragments of his spirit among us." As a further tribute, Murray later published a family memoir entitled Proud Shoes—a phrase Stephen had used more than once.[447] In "Listen to the People," for example, he describes Democracy as "the walker in proud shoes."[448]

The day after his funeral, Rosemary returned to Stephen's desk. "Grief is an agony," she wrote under the last entry he had written in his diary. "But, alas, you don't die of it." Because the following day would be the twenty-second anniversary of their engagement, she added, "My real life . . . began and ended at this time of year."[449]

On March 27, *The Saturday Review of Literature*, the magazine brother William had helped found in 1924, published a memorial issue. In May, Stephen was awarded the Gold Medal for Literature from the National Institute of Arts and Letters. In July, all that he had written of *Western Star* was published. The book reached a national audience and received national honors. It was a Book-of-the-Month Club selection and earned Stephen his second Pulitzer Prize for Poetry.[450]

On April 5, *Life Magazine* honored Stephen with a full-page editorial. *Life* called Stephen "the leading poet of his generation," perhaps, because:

> His home was not any particular town. In a literal sense he belonged to the United States. The deep green valleys of the Delaware, the red rocks of Colorado, the subtle perfumes of California . . . these were his home—*all* of them, passionately. (Emphasis in original)

In each war with which Stephen was linked, *Life* explained—the Civil War via *John Brown's Body* and World Wars I and II—Stephen "performed a miracle: he gave it meaning." Stephen fought with words rather than with bullets, *Life* concluded. Rather than striving to capture ground, Stephen sought to cast a light: "the light of America shining out across a ruined world."[451]

In June of 1943, Stephen received a significant tribute to his service to his country. During that month the Liberty ship *Stephen Vincent Benét* was built and launched.[452]

A Liberty ship similar to the one named for Stephen.

In 1945, many of Stephen's radio scripts were published in a book. These scripts were "written in battle" the introduction explains, "in the hard language of battle," and they were written by "an honest man who [spoke] his truth."[453]

In 1960, Stephen's biographer Charles Fenton also saw Stephen as a soldier. In a collection of Stephen's letters, Fenton says of Stephen's death: "he had been killed in uniform as surely as if he had been burned up in a B-17 or fallen at Guadalcanal."[454]

Over time, Stephen's books faded from bestseller lists and his words no longer filled the airwaves. Still, on his 100th birthday in 1998, a United States postage stamp was issued in his honor.

Ironically, although he struggled for money throughout his life, Stephen's death left his family with a nice financial cushion. Over the years, no matter how little money he had, he'd always paid his life insurance premium. At his death, his family received $57,000 in insurance proceeds—more than $785,000 in today's money.[455] More help for the widow came when Stephen's Uncle Larry Benét died a few years later. With his wife gone and having no children, Uncle Larry left his estate to his favorite relative—Rosemary.[456] Rosemary also earned money as a reader for the Book-of-the-Month Club, a job she eventually chose to do year-round in the family's beloved home in Stonington.[457]

* * *

Several months before his death, Stephen seemed to have sensed what was coming. Receiving a pre-publication version of his two-volume selected works in early 1942, he wrote in his diary: "A very handsome tombstone." In the fall of that year, on a Sunday afternoon, while sitting with his good friend Philip Barry, author of "The Philadelphia Story," on the porch of Barry's East Hampton home, the two talked of epitaphs—words written or said about a person after he dies. "I know what yours should be," Barry said. "Even Stephen." Stephen said: "I like that." And Barry elaborated: "Even Stephen? *He* must go? Even Stephen. Even So." Benét smiled, saying he liked that too—"but it's sort of scary."[458]

Stephen had not been afraid to address death in his work. He had even written a short story back in 1937 where death is a man called "The Fool-Killer."[459] Another mention comes in these words from William Sycamore:

> And my youth returns, like the rains of Spring,
> And my sons, like wild-geese flying
> And I lie and hear the meadow-lark sing
> And have much content in my dying.[460]

Interestingly, Stephen died on the same day as J. Pierpont Morgan, the son of the Gilded Age financier and one of the world's wealthiest men. One newspaper reporting the two deaths referred to the men as "a prince of words and a prince of finance." Most significantly, the reporter reminds his readers that there are various ways to measure wealth when he writes that both men, each in his own way, "were enormously rich."[461]

Philip Barry's *Yale Yearbook* photo. Barry wrote the play "The Philadelphia Story" for actress Katharine Hepburn and was a lifelong friend of Stephen's after the two met in college.

In the years since Stephen's death, his name—once said with reverence by presidents and known by nearly every school-age child in America—has almost been completely forgotten. Yet his work touched our world in so many ways. His words, poems and stories—"Bury My Heart at Wounded Knee," *John Brown's Body*, "Freedom Is a Hard Bought Thing," "The American Dream"—have seeped into our culture, continuing to impact us in ways we may not even be aware.

Yale Series of Younger Poets—Winners

1932-1942[f]

1932 Paul Engle
1933 Shirley Barker
1934 James Agee
1935 Muriel Rukeyser
1936 Edward Weismiller
1937 Margaret Haley
1938 Joy Davidman
1939 Reuel Denney
1940 Norman Rosten
1941 Jeremy Ingalls
1942 Margaret Walker

---
f. Stephen Vincent Benét was the sole judge 1933-1942.

BIBLIOGRAPHY

Benét, Laura. *Famous Poets For Young People*. New York: Dodd, Mead & Company, 1964 ("Famous Poets").

—*When William Rose, Stephen Vincent and I Were Young*. New York: Dodd, Mead & Company, 1976 ("Laura").

—"Laura Benét's Family Photograph Album," unpublished, now in the collection of the Benicia Historical Museum ("Laura's Album").

—"Laura Benét's Scrapbook," unpublished, owned by Tom Benét, reviewed by the author in July 2015 ("Laura's Scrapbook").

Bacon, Leonard. *Semi-Centennial*. New York: Harper & Brothers, 1939 ("Bacon").

Benét, Stephen Vincent. *America*. New York: Farrar & Rinehart, 1944.

—*The Beginning of Wisdom*. New York: Henry Holt and Company, 1921.

—*Cheers for Miss Bishop* (1941)—Screenplay Adaptation by Benét based on Bess Streeter Aldrich's novel *Miss Bishop*, United Artists.

—*The Devil and Daniel Webster and Other Writings*, edited by Townsend Ludington. New York: Penguin Books, 1999 ("Ludington").

—"Freedom From Fear." *The Saturday Evening Post*, March 13, 1943.

—"Freedom's A Hard Bought Thing." *Saturday Evening Post*, May 18, 1940.

—*James Shore's Daughter*. Garden City: Doubleday, Doran & Company 1934.

—*John Brown's Body*. New York: Rinehart & Company, 1954.

—"The Most Unforgettable Character I've Met." *The Reader's Digest*, October 1940: 113-116 ("Character").

—"My Favorite Fiction Character." *The Bookman,* 62, No. 6 (February 1926) 672-673 ("Fiction Character").

—*Selected Works of Stephen Vincent Benét, Volume One: Poetry* ("Selected Works--Poetry") *Volume Two: Prose* ("Selected Works—Prose") New York: Farrar & Rinehart 1942.

—"The Sixth Man." *Breaking Into Print*, edited by Elmer Adler. New York: Simon and Schuster 1937.

—*Thirteen O'clock and Other Stories*.

—*We Stand United and Other Radio Scripts*. New York: Farrar & Rinehart 1945 ("Radio Scripts").

—*Western Star*. New York: Farrar & Rinehart 1943 ("Western Star").

Benét, Stephen Vincent and Rosemary Carr Benét. *A Book of Americans*. New York: Henry Holt and Company 1933.

Benét, Thomas Carr, interview with author, November 2001.
—Interviews with author, July 2015.
—"Speech to Town and Country Club," unpublished manuscript, (undated) ("Tom Benét Speech").
—Transcript of "Thomas C. Benét appearance at the Benicia Historical Museum" (1/24/1995) Benicia, California, unpublished manuscript ("Benicia Talk").

Benét, William Rose. "My Brother Steve" in "Stephen Vincent Benét," published by *The Saturday Review of Literature* and Farrar & Rinehart, 1943 ("William").
—*The Dust Which is God.* New York: Dodd Mead & Co. 1941 ("Dust").

Dillon, Richard. *Great Expectations—The Story of Benicia, California*. Fresno: Benicia Heritage Book 1980.

Edwards, Anne. *Road to Tara*. New York: Dell Publishing Company 1983.

Farrar, John "For the Record" in "Stephen Vincent Benét," published by *The Saturday Review of Literature* and Farrar & Rinehart 1943 ("Farrar").

Fenton, Charles A. *Stephen Vincent Benét—The Life and Times of an American Man of Letters 1898-1943*. New Haven: Yale University Press 1958 ("Fenton").
—, ed. *Selected Letters of Stephen Vincent Benét*. New Haven: Yale University Press 1960 (*"Letters"*).

"Hammonds Railroad and Trade Centers Map of the United States and Canada, West" 1906.

Hively, Evelyn Helmick *Darling Ro and the Benét Women*. Kent: Kent State University Press 2011 ("Hively").

Life Editorial. "Stephen Benét—The Ultimate Objectives of Free Men Are to be Discovered in Their Arts and Letters." *Life*. April 5, 1943: 22 ("*Life* Editorial").

Murray, James V. and John Swantek, editors and compilers. *The Watervliet Arsenal—A Chronology of the Nation's Oldest Arsenal*. Watervliet: Watervliet Public Affairs Office 1993 ("Watervliet").

Norris, Kathleen. *Family Gathering* (Hardcover). New York: Doubleday & Co. 1959 ("Norris-1").
-*Family Gathering* (Paperback). New York: Paperback Library, 1971 ("Norris-2").

"Once Whistler's, Now Benét's." *House & Garden*. November 1942: 36-37.

Schauffler, Edward. A. "Stephen Vincent Benét A Poet who Served a Cause With 'Bright Valor'" *Kansas City Star*. March 15,1943 ("Schauffler").

Schorer, Mark. *Sinclair Lewis, An American Life*. New York: McGraw-Hill Book Company, 1961 ("Schorer").

Wold, Gladys. *Benicia History and Historical Guide (1971)*.

NOTES

1. *Margaret Mitchell's* Gone With the Wind *Letters*, 1936–1949, Richard Harwell, ed. (New York: MacMillan, Inc., 1976) Margaret Mitchell to SVB July 9, 1936, pages 34–36.

2. Laura 62–63.

3. Thomas, David "The Changing of a Paradigm: The Case for Health Care," The University of New South Wales sphcm.med.unsw.edu.au/.../GENM0518_...Changing-paradigm.pdf (circa 2008) accessed July, 2015.

4. Laura 60.

5. Id. 61–62.

6. Id. 70.

7. Fenton, Illustration 3a. Also photos in the Thomas C. Benét Collection.

8. Watervliet 145–146.

9. Laura 74.

10. Fenton 8.

11. *Letters* 82 (emphasis in original).

12. Laura 86.

13. Ibid.

14. *Famous Poets* 130.

15. Laura 88.

16. *Western Star*.

17. *Sixth Man* 23

18. Laura 88.

19. Bacon 116.

20. Laura 88.

21. Fenton 9.

22   Character 114.
23   William 3.
24   Schorer 152.
25   Laura's Album.
26   Fenton 17.
27   Book-of-the-Month Club brochure for July and August, 1942.
28   Benicia Talk.
29   Laura 93–94.
30   Norris-2 49–50.
31   Handwritten notation by Susan Talmadge in a copy of *1920 Blue and Gold*, yearbook of the University of California at Berkeley.
32   The information about Sinclair Lewis is from: Fenton 3 and 57 and Schorer.
33   Schorer 159.
34   "To W.R.B. Dedication" by SVB in *Young Adventure*, Yale University Press, 1918.
35   The information about the *Solano* is from: Laura 9, William 5 and Wold, *Benicia History and Historical Guide* (1971).
36   Fenton 8.
37   William 2.
38   Fenton 6.
39   The information about SVB's reading is from Fenton 6–8 and 31–34, William 3–4 and Laura 100.
40   Farrar 14.
41   SVB letter to "Tom Graham" (August, 1912) via Fenton 31–35.
42   Laura 80.
43   Laura 101.
44   "Marrying." Original typed page by SVB in the Thomas C. Benét Collection, reviewed by author, July, 2015. Spelling and punctuation are Stephen's.

45. William 1.

46. Jomini's *Political and Military History of the Campaign of Waterloo* translated by Stephen Vincent Benét (New York, 1853); General Benét also translated "Military Law and the Practice of Courts-Martial" (1862), and "Electro-Ballistic Machines and the Schultze Chronoscope" (1866).

47. Copy of General Stephen Vincent Benét's translation of Jomini's *Political and Military History of the Campaign of Waterloo* (New York, 1853), inscribed, owned by Tom Benét, viewed by the author on June 16, 2015.

48. Schorer 152

49. Sixth Man 23.

50. Laura 42.

51. Information about *Minus Poetry*: Fenton 11.

52. Laura 89.

53. Sixth Man 25–26.

54. Margaret's wedding, Norris-2 104.

55. Boarding school, Fenton 15–20.

56. Laura 94.

57. The information about SVB's donkey and cart is from Laura 91–93.

58. Fenton 27–28.

59. Fenton 15.

60. "James Walker Benét, Colonel, United States Army," Arlington National Cemetery Website, accessed March, 2015.

61. "Even in the lion's cage . . . " SVB, "Sparrow" (1936), *Selected Works—Poetry* 416.

62. Fenton 23.

63. Fenton 22.

64. See *Dust* 122–125.

65. Schauffler, no page number as found in Laura's Scrapbook, and Tom Benét Speech 1.

66. Fenton 25–26.

67 Fenton 28–29.

68 Fenton 27.

69 "The Mountain Whippoorwill" (1925), *Selected Works—Poetry* 376.

70 Fenton 33.

71 Fenton 32.

72 Fenton 33.

73 Character 113.

74 SVB, poem in *St. Nicholas Magazine* (September 1912) via Fenton 35.

75 Fenton 37.

76 Fenton 38.

77 Sixth Man 27.

78 Fenton 40–42.

79 Fenton 43–44.

80 SVB "The Retort Discourteous" (1920), *Selected Works—Poetry* 387.

81 Binder, Eve "You Would Never Have Gotten Into Harvard in 1899" www.ivygateblog.com12011/04 accessed July 25, 2015.

82 Id. Quoting Thomas Rhiel describing Columbia's 1899 Entrance Exam.

83 Fenton 52.

84 SVB "Three Day's Ride," *Yale Literary Magazine* 81(1915–16) via Fenton 383, n. 7.

85 "Three Days Ride" (1920), *Selected Works—Poetry* 389.

86 Fenton 56–57.

87 "The Drug Shop or Endymion in Edmonstoun," *Young Adventure*, Yale University Press (New Haven 1918) see also www.poetryarchive.com.

88 Prefatory Note to "The Drug Shop" at www.readbookonline.net/readOnLine/46668/ accessed July, 2015.

89 Fenton 51.

90   Information about Farrar: Fenton 53 and Farrar.

91   Banks, Arthur *A Military Atlas of the First World War*, Heinemann Educational Books Ltd. (Great Britain, 1975) "German Cartographic Propaganda, 1915" 132.

92   Fenton 66.

93   Information about war practice at Yale: Fenton 69 and Farrar 33.

94   SVB "Scholastic Work is Still the Most Important Thing at Yale," *Yale Record*, 46 (12/14/1917) 55 via Fenton 66.

95   "KP" Fenton 73 referencing Robert Van Gelder, "Mr. Benét's Work in Progress," *New York Times Book Review*, 6 (April 21, 1940), 20; see also *Life* Editorial.

96   Fenton 73–74.

97   Fenton 76–77.

98   Fenton 77.

99   Fenton 78; for info about Fitzgerald see "F. Scott Fitzgerald" entry "Zelda" section, en.wikipedia.org/wiki/F._Scott_Fitzgerald, accessed July 25, 2015.

100   Fenton 78.

101   SVB, "Lunch Time on Broadway," *Heavens and Earth* (1920) 41 via Fenton 81.

102   Fenton 81.

103   Fenton 81–82.

104   "Stephen Vincent Benét" Wikipedia citing *The New Encyclopedia Britannica*, Vol. 12, Micropaedia, 15th edition, Encyclopedia Britannica Inc. c. 1989, accessed November 14, 2014.

105   Fenton 91.

106   "Dulce Ridentem" (1925), *Selected Works—Poetry* 361.

107   Fenton 81.

108   See front and back endpapers of Norris-1 for a Thompson family tree and Norris-2 120.

109   *The Beginning of Wisdom* 92¬–93.

110   SVB to George Abbe (4/14/1939) via Fenton 92–97.

111 Fenton 96–97.

112 James Walker Benét to Odus Creamer Horney (March 5, 1921) via Fenton 97.

113 "L.V. Benét Dies; Invented Hotchkiss Gun," *New York Times* (5/22/1948); "Hotchkiss M1914 Machine Gun" en.wikipedia.org/wiki/Hotchkiss_M1914_machine_gun accessed August 7, 2015.

114 Fenton 98.

115 Fenton 99.

116 Fenton 99–100.

117 Fenton 102.

118 Fenton 103–104.

119 *Dust* 344.

120 "Difference" (1921), *Selected Works—Poetry* 355.

121 "A Nonsense Song" (1925), *Selected Works—Poetry* 356.

122 "Bunches of Grapes" by Walter De la Mare (1902), www.public-domain-poetry.com/walter-de-la-mare/bunches... accessed August 6, 2015. Also Hively 11.

123 Fenton 103.

124 Ludington x–xi.

125 Fenton 104–105.

126 Floyd Gibbons, editor of the *Chicago Tribune*, to Rosemary Carr, via Tom Benét Interview with author, November 2001.

127 Fenton 106.

128 Fenton 106–107.

129 Fenton 108–109.

130 Fenton 107.

131 William Benét, *First Person Singular* (New York: George H. Doran Company 1922) iv.

132 Fenton 107.

133 Woods, Brenda "The Third Benét," *Modern Maturity Magazine* (February–March 1978) 15.

134. Fenton 107.
135. Fenton 109.
136. Fenton 106 and 107–108.
137. Fenton 108.
138. Fenton 116.
139. Fenton 108.
140. Carl Brandt to Rosemary Benét (March 15, 1943) via Fenton 108–109.
141. Fenton 110.
142. Fenton 112.
143. Brandt's advice: Carl Brandt to Fenton, interview (January 26, 1955) via Fenton 111-113.
144. Fenton 114–115.
145. Fenton 116–117.
146. Fenton 119.
147. Fenton 117–118.
148. SVB, "The Ballad of William Sycamore" (1922), *Selected Works—Poetry* 370.
149. Fenton 120.
150. Fenton 122–124.
151. Fenton 125.
152. $125 to $200 in 1922 would be about $1700 to $2800 in 2015 dollars.
153. Fenton 133.
154. Fenton 124.
155. Fenton 128.
156. "The Ballad of William Sycamore" (1922), *Selected Works—Poetry* 368–370.
157. Fenton 128.

158 Young, Steve "The Ballad of William Sycamore" on *Solo/Live* Released March 1991; "Steve Young 'The Ballad of William Sycamore' (from Benét poem)" on YouTube at: https://youtu.be/YhpI0LL9Byk accessed July 28, 2015.

159 "Elinor Wylie," Wikipedia https://en.wikipedia.org/wiki/Elinor_Wylie accessed July 25, 2015.

160 For an excellent history of the *Saturday Review of Literature* see http://www.things-and-other-stuff.com/magazines/saturday-review.html accessed January 18, 2016.

161 Fenton 135.

162 "Margaret O'Neill Eaton," Wikipedia, accessed December 23, 2015.

163 Fenton 140.

164 Fenton 136.

165 Fenton 135–141.

166 Woollcott, Alexander "'Nerves' Played at the Comedy—Shallow Pated War Drama With One Taut Scene," *New York World* (September 2, 1924).

167 $35 in 1924 would be about $488 in 2015 dollars; Fenton 137.

168 Fenton 147.

169 Fenton 295, citing SVB, "The Author is Pleased," *New York Times* (9/28/1941) p. 4.

170 SVB to Elizabeth Manwaring (11/1931) via Fenton 145.

171 Fenton 143.

172 Fenton 223.

173 Fenton 161.

174 Tom Benét Interview with the author, November 2001.

175 Fenton 302.

176 Fenton 303.

177 "Georgia Old Time Fiddler Conventions," *New Georgia Encyclopedia*, www.georgiaencyclopedia.org/articles/arts-culture/georgia-old-time-fiddlers-conventions, accessed 7/2015.

178 Fenton 148.

179 "The Mountain Whippoorwill" (1925), *Selected Works—Poetry* 376.

180   Nitty Gritty Dirt Band *Stars & Stripes Forever*, Album (1974) "The Mountain Whippoorwill (Or How Hillbilly Jim Won the Great Fiddler's Prize)."

181   "'Devil Went Down to Georgia' by the Charlie Daniels Band" on "Songfacts" http://www.songfacts.com/detail.php?id=6547 accessed 7/2015. The song appeared on the *Million Mile Reflections* album (1979). The Grammy the song won was the 1979 Grammy for Best Country Performance by a Duo or Group with Vocal.

182   Steve Martin, *Born Standing Up: A Comic's Life* (New York: Simon and Schuster 2007) 67–68.

183   Fenton 151.

184   Fenton 154–155.

185   Fenton 142.

186   Fenton 159–163.

187   Fenton 164–165.

188   Fenton 168.

189   SVB to Rosemary Benét (1925) via Fenton 158.

190   Fenton 167–168 and "Letters Submitted to the Guggenheim Foundation," Ludington 465.

191   Fenton 167–168.

192   Fiction Character and Fenton 166.

193   Fenton 167–168.

194   Fenton 169–170.

195   "The Sobbin' Women" in Luddington 29.

196   *Seven Brides For Seven Brothers* (1954).

197   Fenton 176.

198   Fenton 177–179.

199   *John Brown's Body* in *Selected Works—Poetry* (hereinafter "*John Brown's Body*") 18.

200   Fenton 180.

201   Fenton 191.

202   *Letters* 217.

203   Fenton 187–189.

204   "American Names" (1927), *Selected Works—Poetry* 367.

205   "American Names" (1927), *Selected Works—Poetry* 368.

206   Brown, Dee *Bury My Heart at Wounded Knee*, New York: Henry Holt and Company (1970).

207   Fenton 183.

208   Fenton 184–185.

209   Fenton 185.

210   Fenton 191.

211   Fenton 199.

212   Fenton 194.

213   Fenton 203.

214   Fenton 201–202.

215   Fenton 202.

216   Fenton 203.

217   *John Brown's Body* 4.

218   *John Brown's Body* 7.

219   *John Brown's Body* 8.

220   *John Brown's Body* 88.

221   *John Brown's Body* 89.

222   *John Brown's Body* 92.

223   *John Brown's Body* 144.

224   *John Brown's Body* 196.

225   *John Brown's Body* 328.

226   *John Brown's Body* 336.

227 Fenton 211.

228 *Letters* 172; also quoted slightly differently in Fenton 212.

229 Fenton 212–213.

230 About $348,000 in 2015 dollars, Fenton 220.

231 About $7,000 to $14,000 in 2015 dollars, Fenton 220.

232 Fenton 220.

233 Margaret Mitchell to Clifford Dowdy (July 29, 1937). Incident also mentioned in letter from MM to SVB (July 1936). Daniel identified in his article in the *Atlanta Journal* (7/21/1940) via *Road to Tara* 146.

234 "John Brown's Body Hits the Road" *Colliers*, December 6, 1952.

235 Friedlander, Benjamin "Hayden's Epic of Community" *Modern American Poetry* www.english.illinois.edu/maps/poets/g_l/hayden/hayden accessed August 7, 2015.

236 "Robert Hayden" *Academy of American Poets* www.poets.org/poetsorg/poet/robert-hayden accessed August 7, 2015.

237 Coates, Ta-Nehisi, *Between the World and Me* (New York: Spiegal&Grau, 2015) 51.

238 "Transcript: Senator Edward M. Kennedy Reads his Favorite Poems" from "Poets and the Creative Mind" an American Academy of Poets event, April 6, 2004 http://www.poets.org/poetsorg/text/transcript-senator-edward-m-kennedy-reads-his-favorite-poems accessed July 31, 2015.

239 Tom Benét Speech 3.

240 Tom Benét, Speech 3, and "Man charged in Theft of JFK Jr. Belongings," AP report in the *Cape Cod Times* (April 15, 2004).

241 Conversation with Tom Benét, June 2002; www.johnbrownsbodyfilm.com accessed July 27, 2015.

242 Fenton 220–221.

243 "Annotated Edition," the opening poem in *The Last Circle*. See also Fenton 221–222.

244 Fenton 229–230.

245 *James Shore's Daughter* 142.

246 Elinor Wylie, "Love to Stephen" from *Last Poems of Elinor Wylie* published by Alfred A. Knopf as reprinted with permission in the *The Saturday Review of Literature* March 27, 1943.

247 Norris-2 146–151.

248 Brenda Woods, "The Third Benét," *Modern Maturity Magazine* (February–March 1978) 15.

249 Fenton 231.

250 Fenton 146.

251 Fenton 233 and Gish, Lillian *D.W. Griffith Book* via Tom Benét Speech 4.

252 *Abraham Lincoln* (1930 film), Wikipedia, en.wikipedia.org/wiki/Abraham_Lincoln_(1930_film) accessed August 9, 2015.

253 Fenton 233, and Tom Benét Speech 4–5.

254 Ludington xxvii.

255 *Letters* 192–195.

256 Ibid.

257 SVB to Rosemary Benét (December 1929) via Ludington, xxvii.

258 SVB to Carl Brandt (1/1930) via Fenton 236 and Ludington xxvii.

259 Fenton 239–240.

260 Tom Benét Speech 5.

261 Abraham Lincoln (D.W.Griffith) 1930 Full Movie, www.youtube.com/watch?v=1FfcCWonACo accessed August 9, 2015.

262 Fenton 240.

263 Fenton 241.

264 "Health Insurance in the United States," https://en.wikipedia.org/wiki/Health_insurance_in_the_United_States accessed July 30, 2015.

265 Fenton 245.

266 Fenton 247.

267 Fenton 246–247.

268 Fenton 247.

269 Fenton 249.

270 Tom Benét Speech 7.

271 Fenton 249–250.

272 Fenton 286.

273 Fenton 250.

274 For each lecture, circa 1932, he would be paid between $100 and $350, the equivalent of $1700 to $6,000 in 2015 dollars.

275 Fenton 303–304.

276 Fenton 250–251.

277 Fenton 252.

278 *Letters* 369.

279 Fenton 252.

280 "Complaint of Body, the Ass, Against his Rider, the Soul" (1936), *Selected Works—Poetry* 418.

281 *Letters* 238.

282 SVB to Paul Engle (9/1933) via Fenton 255.

283 Fenton 255–257.

284 "Captain Kidd," *Book of Americans* 25 (emphasis in original).

285 "Woodrow Wilson," *Book of Americans* 113. Still another person with his own poem in this book is Johnny Appleseed. Appleseed's poem now reaches children in a new form. In 2001, this poem became a children's picture book, illustrated by S.D. Schindler. *Johnny Appleseed* written by SVB, illustrated by S.D. Schindler; Margaret K. McElderry Books (New York, 2001).

286 Famous Poets 133.

287 "Yale Series of Younger Poets," http://yalepress.yale.edu/yupbooks/SeriesPage.asp?Series=113 accessed September 12, 2015, and *Letters* 341.

288 Fenton 260.

289 Fenton 264–265.

290 *Letters* 226–229; https://en.wikipedia.org/wiki/Shirley_Barker accessed September 12, 2015.

291 *Letters* 245–246; https://en.wikipedia.org/wiki/James_Agee accessed September 12, 2015.

292 *Letters* 244–248; https://en.wikipedia.org/wiki/Muriel_Rukeyser accessed September 12, 2015.

293 https://en.wikipedia.org/wiki/Joy_Davidman and https://en.wikipedia.org/wiki/C._S._Lewis accessed September 12, 2015, and Letters 340.

294 Fenton 264.

295 Tom Benét Speech 6.

296 "Margaret Walker," en.wikipedia.org/wiki/Margaret_Walker accessed 8/24/2015.

297 "Margaret Walker," en.wikipedia.org/wiki/Margaret_Walker accessed 8/7/2015.

298 Margaret Walker, *Jubilee* (New York: Bantam Books, 1966) cover blurbs.

299 Tom Benét Speech 6–7.

300 Fenton 260; *Letters* 236–253; Richard B. Weber, "Paul Engle: A Checklist" http://ir.uiowa.edu/cgi/viewcontent.cgi?article=1035&context=bai accessed September 12, 2015;

301 *Letters* 252.

302 "Paul Engle," https://en.wikipedia.org/wiki/Paul_Engle accessed September 13, 2015, and "Paul Engle," http://www.writinguniversity.org/author/paul-engle accessed September 14, 2015.

303 "Biography of Paul Engle," http://www.poemhunter.com/paul-engle/biography/ accessed 11/11/2015.

304 Fenton 265; *Letters* 232.

305 Fenton 268.

306 Fenton 269.

307 Fenton 273

308 Fenton 267; *Letters* 132.

309 Tom Benét Interview with the Author, November 2001.

310 SVB Diary (1933) via Fenton 281.

311 Fenton 282.

312 "Books: Golden Honeymoon," *Time Magazine* (January 28, 1935).

313 Fenton 284–286.

314 "If This Should Change," Ludington 481.

315 "Freedom From Fear," *The Saturday Evening Post* (March 13, 1943) no page number.

316 Fenton 275.

317 *Burning City* (New York: Farrar & Rinehart, 1936).

318 "Notes to Be Left in a Cornerstone" (1936), *Selected Works—Poetry* 423.

319 Later called "By the Waters of Babylon," *Selected Works—Prose* 471.

320 Id. 480–481.

321 SVB "Nightmare Number Three" (1935), *Selected Works—Poetry* 452.

322 Andre Maurois, *Patapoufs et Filifers*, trans. Rosemary Benét (New York: Henry Holt, 1940) via Tom Benét Speech 7.

323 Fenton 290.

324 Fenton 290.

325 Fenton 291.

326 "The Devil and Daniel Webster," *Selected Works—Prose* (hereinafter "The Devil and Daniel Webster") 32.

327 Rosemary Benét, "Advice to My Daughter"; Tom Benét Speech 7.

328 Tom Benét Speech 7.

329 Tom Benét Speech 9.

330 Tom Benét Interview with the Author, November 2001.

331 Tom Benét Interview with the Author, July 23, 2015.

332 Tom Benét Speech 10.

333 Fenton 291.

334 Fenton 291.

335 Fenton 292.

336 "The Devil and Daniel Webster" 33.

337 "The Devil and Daniel Webster" 37.

338 Id. 41.

339 Id. 42–43.

340 "The Devil and Daniel Webster" 26.

341 Fenton 293–294.

342 "John Huston," https://en.wikipedia.org/wiki/John_Huston#Awards_and_honors, accessed December 28, 2015.

343 Under the title *Shortcut to Happiness*, released on DVD outside the United States in 2010.

344 Fenton 293–296.

345 *Letters* 294.

346 The equivalent of two or three thousand dollars in 1936.

347 Fenton 296.

348 Fenton 353.

349 "Introduction" in *Letters* vii–xxiv.

350 $15,000 in 1937 would be worth just over $248,000 in 2015.

351 Fenton 342.

352 Tom Benét Speech 6.

353 SVB "chained-smoked while he worked" Fenton 191.

354 *Letters* 208.

355 Fenton 343–344.

356 Fenton 345–346 and 350 and *Western Star*.

357 Fenton 344; Ludington, back cover.

358 *Western Star* vii.

360 *Western Star* 56.

361 Fenton 349.

362 Fenton 348.

363 Fenton 344.
364 Fenton 340.
365 Fenton 348–349.
366 Fenton 353.
367 "They Burned the Books," *Radio Scripts* 102.
368 Fenton 353.
369 Fenton 359–360.
370 Fenton 360–361; *Letters* 388.
371 Fenton 360–361; Wiley, Mason and Damien Bona, *Inside Oscar* (New York: Ballantine Books, 1987) 106.
372 "United We Stand," *Radio Scripts* 5–6.
373 SVB Diary (November 7, 1940) via Fenton 361.
374 "Nightmare at Noon" (1940), *Selected Works—Poetry* 464.
375 Fenton 362–363.
376 Farrar 28–29 quoting Milton Krentz, Radio Director for the Council for Democracy.
377 "Listen to the People," *Selected Works—Poetry* 481–482.
378 "Listen to the People," *Selected Works—Poetry* 481.
379 "Listen to the People," *Selected Works—Poetry* 481 and Farrar 29.
380 *Letters* 392.
381 Fenton 363.
382 Fenton 364.
383 *Western Star*, v.
384 Fenton 364.
385 Fenton 364–365.
386 "Freedom's A Hard Bought Thing," *Selected Works—Prose* 46.

387 Fenton 365.

388 O. Henry Awards List, https://en.wikipedia.org/wiki/O._Henry_Award accessed July 15, 2015; Farrar 26.

389 Martin Luther King, Jr., "Testament of Hope" in *A Testament of Hope—The Essential Writings and Speeches of Martin Luther King, Jr.*, edited by James Melville (Washington, San Francesco: HarperCollins 1991) 314–315.

390 Pauli Murray, *Proud Shoes* (Boston: Beacon Press, 1999) back cover. "Pauli Murray" in Isabel V. Morin, *Women Who Reformed Politics* (Minneapolis, MN: Oliver Press, 1994).

391 Patricia Bell-Scott, *The Firebrand and the First Lady: Portrait of a Friendship* (New York: Knopf, Doubleday 2016.)

392 "Two Letters to Paulie Murray" in Ludington 479. These quotations are from an undated letter in response to Murray's letter to SVB of April 17, 1940.

393 Fenton 366.

394 Fenton 368.

395 "The American Dream," *The Country Gentleman* (November 1942) no page number, as found in Laura's Scrapbook.

396 Coates 116.

397 Joshua Zeitz, "*Born to Run* and the Decline of the American Dream," *The Atlantic* (September 2015).

398 Schauffler, no page number, as found in Laura's Scrapbook.

399 "Listen to the People," *Selected works—Poetry* 487.

400 "A Creed for Americans," written for the Council for Democracy, 285 Madison Avenue, NY, no date.

401 *The Country Gentleman* (November 1942).

402 "A Child is Born," *Radio Scripts* 176.

403 *Letters* 389 and https://en.wikipedia.org/wiki/Carl_Sandburg accessed July 2015.

404 *James Shores' Daughter* 264.

405 *Letters* 389.

406 Farrar 31.

407 "They Burned the Books," *Radio Scripts* 110.

408 "They Burned the Books," *Radio Scripts* 204, and "Prayer" 210.

409 Farrar 30.

410 *Radio Scripts* 10.

411 "Housewife and Mother," *Radio Scripts* 40–41.

412 "Housewife and Mother," *Radio Scripts* 44.

413 Fenton 371.

414 *Life Magazine* (July 27, 1942) 74–79.

415 "Stephen V. Benét and the American Past," review of *Selected Works of Stephen by Vincent Benét*, by Joseph Wood Krutch (Professor of English, Columbia University), *New York Herald Tribune* (June 21, 1942) no page number, as found in Laura's Scrapbook.

416 "Once Whistler's, Now Benét's," *House & Garden* (November 1942): 36–37; also mentioned in Fenton 371–372 and William 9.

417 *Letters* 363–364 and "Cheers for Miss Bishop," https://en.wikipedia.org/wiki/Cheers_for_Miss_Bishop accessed August 2015.

418 Farrar 36.

419 "A Child is Born," *Radio Scripts* 178–179.

420 "The Pulitzer Prizes: Winners by Year," www.pulitzer.org/awards/1942 accessed July 2015.

421 "Elinor Wylie 1885–1928," Poetry Foundation, http://www.poetryfoundation.org/bio/elinor-wylie accessed July 30, 2015.

422 *Life* Editorial.

423 Fenton 371.

424 Fenton 372.

425 Fenton 372 and *America*.

426 Fenton 372.

427 Farrar 22.

428 Farrar 35.

429 SVB Diary (March 9, 1943) via Fenton 373.

430 "Prayer," *Radio Scripts* 209–210.

431 Farrar 35.

432 Via Fenton 373 and Tom Benét Speech—the Benét family occasionally played charades.

433 "Freedom From Fear" no page number. The other three Freedoms: Of Religion, Of Speech and From Want ("Four Freedoms: (Norman Rockwell)" https://en.wikipedia.org/wiki/Four_Freedoms_%28Norman_Rockwell%29 accessed January 9, 2016.

434 Fenton 219.

435 "The Joos Ballet Chronicles The Nightmares of a Dictator" *PM Weekly* (October 17, 1941) no page number, as found in Laura's Scrapbook.

436 "Movies Present 'The Devil vs. Daniel Webster'" *PM Weekly* (October 19, 1941) no page number, as found in Laura's Scrapbook.

437 Fenton 373.

438 "Memory" 1936 *Selected Works—Poetry* 364.

439 Notes for "The Watchers By the Stone" via Farrar 35.

440 Tom Benét Interview with the Author, November 2001.

441 Fenton 8.

442 Fenton 373.

443 Ludington ix.

444 "Schauffler," no page number.

445 Joy Davidman, "Stephen Vincent Benét," *New Masses Review* (March 30, 1943) no page number, as found in Laura's Scrapbook.

446 Jan Struther, "Stephen Vincent Benét, July 22, 1898–March 13, 1943," reprinted in "Books and Things" ed. Lewis Gannett, *New York Herald Tribune* (March 27, 1943) no page number, as found in Laura's Scrapbook.

447 Ludington xxviii–xxix.

448 "Listen to the People," *Selected Works—Poetry* 485.

449 SVB Diary, entry by Rosemary Benét (March 16, 1943) via Fenton 373.

450 Fenton 374; Pulitzer Prize List http://www.pulitzer.org/bycat accessed July, 30, 2015.

451 *Life* Editorial.

452 "List of Liberty Ships S-A," Wikipedia, https://en.wikipedia.org/wiki/List_of_Liberty_ships_(S%E2%80%93Z) accessed 7/30/2015; see also Fenton, illustration 12.b.

453 Norman Rosten, "Forward," *Radio Scripts* viii.

454 *Letters* 362.

455 Fenton 373.

456 Conversation with Tom Benét June 16, 2015.

457 Tom Benét Speech 9.

458 Fenton 367–368.

459 "Johnny Pye and the Fool-Killer" (1937), *Selected Works—Prose* 90.

460 "William Sycamore," *Selected Works—Poetry* 370.

461 "Two Noted Americans Die," unsigned, undated news clipping from unknown newspaper, circa March 14, 1943, in unpublished Laura Benét Scrapbook, owned by Tom Benét, reviewed by the author in July 2015.

Photo Credits

"Father James Walker Benét and Mother Frances Rose Benét," Tom Benét.

"The Benét Family home in Watervliet," HABS Survey--Library of Congress, Prints & Photographs Division, HABS, Reproduction number HABS NY,1-WAVL,1/2—1.

"Stephen in a 16 inch gun," Tom Benét.

"The big house with the big porch and all California outside," Tom Benét.

"Laura, Stephen and William," Tom Benét.

"Cover of *Hike and the Aeroplane*," first published 1912, public domain.

"Grandfather Stephen Vincent Benét and Grandmother Laura Walker Benét," Tom Benét.

"A cover of *St. Nicholas Magazine* in 1910," public domain.

"Stephen with donkey and cart," Tom Benét.

"The Benét home at the Augusta Arsenal was another pillared mansion," Donnell Rubay.

"Stephen had time to attend the movies every week," public domain.

"Yale University, 1915," public domain. File:Rummell, Richard Yale University.jpg Wikimedia Commons.

"Stephen's *Yale Yearbook* photo," Wikimedia Commons.

"Greetings From the City of New York", mailed 1907, public domain.

"Two views of the Commanding Officer's Quarters at Watervliet," from HABS Survey Library of Congress, Prints & Photographs Division, HABS, Reproduction number HABS NY,1-WAVL,1/1—1 and HABS NY,1-WAVL,1/1--3.

"*The Beginning of Wisdom*, Stephen's first novel," first published 1921, public domain.

"Stephen and Rosemary around the time of their engagement," Tom Benét.

"Stephen spent his time in that hot garage with a typewriter like this one," Library of Congress, Prints & Photographs Division, FSA/OWI Collection, LC-USF34-026046-C.

"*Harper's Bazaar* cover for August, 1920," public domain.

"Covers from *Cosmopolitan Magazine* and *The Ladies' Home Journal* from the early 1920s." public domain.

"John Farrar–Stephen's college pal," from the *Yale Graphic* which ended publication sometime in 1922 or earlier

(*Yale Banner & Potpourri* 1921-1922, p. 122) public domain.

"Posters for two of D.W. Griffith's silent movies," public domain.

"Stephen and friend," Tom Benét.

"New York Public Library," public domain NYC_Public_Library_postcard_1920.jpg Wiki Commons.

The tip of New York City's Manhattan Island, circa 1942; U.S. National Archives Original file: american_cities_047.jpg National Archives (AMCITY #47.)

"Clockwise from left, unknown British (?) officer, Stephanie, Rosemary, Stephen, Tom and Rachel," Tom Benét.

"The style of printer and keyboard combo, also known as a 'typewriter', which Stephen used in the 1930's," Donnell Rubay.

"An early World War II recruitment poster," Avenge_Pearl_Harbor-Our_Bullets_Will_Do_It.jpg (371 × 574 pixels, file size: 150 KB, MIME type: image/jpeg.)

"'The Whistler House,' home of Stephen and his family in Stonington, Connecticut," Donnell Rubay.

"Relaxing on the back porch, circa 1940's" Tom Benét

"A Liberty Ship similar to the one named for Stephen," from Library of Congress, Prints & Photographs Division, FSA/OWI Collection, LC-USW33-021111-ZC.

"Philip Barry's *Yale Yearbook* Photo," from the *Yale Graphic*, public domain.

Author photo by Victor Edmonds and Jon Van Landschoot, created by Tom Stanton.

Acknowledgements

Deepest thanks to Tom Benét for sharing his knowledge of his family and allowing the use of quotations and photos in this book, and for weathering with me the years it has taken to complete this book.

Thank you to Scott Argo, Interim Director, Office of Academic Admissions, Georgia Regents University, for allowing me to tour the former Benét home in the former Augusta Arsenal.

Thanks to all those who are part of Benicia Literary Arts for making this book a reality, especially Lois Requist and Jim Stevenson. BLA is a wonderful asset to both the community and the literary world.

Special thanks to Mary Eichbauer, Kathryn Reiss and Dave Badtke, my editors.

And, I can't forget all my helpers at the Benicia Library!

Finally, I must acknowledge Charles Fenton—author of the only adult biography of Stephen Vincent Benét. Because Fenton's book was the only biography, it was an important resource for my own book during the many years of writing. For the bulk of that time I visualized Fenton as a stuffy old professor who delivered boring lectures and spent his free time in a research library. Within the past year, however, I was amazed to learn that Fenton was anything but stuffy, or old, or boring. The man rated his own biography, by Scott Donaldson, called *Death of a Rebel: The Charlie Fenton Story.*

Though Fenton eventually earned his Ph.D. from Yale and became a popular English professor at Yale and Duke, he remained a rebel of sorts all of his life. He began his rebelling early when he was kicked out of Yale. When World War II started, not wishing to wait until America joined the fray, Fenton abandoned his education to become a pilot in the Royal Canadian Air Force. His defiance of authority resulted in his demotion to tail gunner, where he lasted for 24 harrowing missions before rejecting Air Force life and going AWOL for several months in London.

Fenton's rebellious life was cut short by his untimely death at the age of 41 in the summer of 1960.

ABOUT THE AUTHOR

Donnell Rubay is a former lawyer and high school history and English teacher. She is the author of the picture book *Stickeen: John Muir and the Brave Little Dog* (Dawn Publications); the time-travel middle-grade novel *Emma and the Oyster Pirate*; and the historical novel *Liberty's Call: A Story of the American Revolution.*

www.ingramcontent.com/pod-product-compliance
Lightning Source LLC
Chambersburg PA
CBHW080119020526
44112CB00037B/2801